DARK HORSES

The Magazine of Weird Fiction

MARCH | 2025

No. 38

Copyright © 2025 Hobb's End Press. All Rights Reserved. Published by Hobb's End Press, a division of ACME Sprockets & Visions. Cover design Copyright © 2025 Wayne Kyle Spitzer. All stories Copyright © 2025 by their respective authors. Please direct all inquiries to: HobbsEndBooks@yahoo.com

CONTENTS

CODED
Daniel M. Wilson

DREAMS HAVE CONSEQUENCES
Barry Vitcov

I FEEL FINE
Sarah Archer

THE DARK GIFT
Daniel Loebl

BEYOND THE BLACK CURTAIN: AWAKENING
Wayne Kyle Spitzer

THE DOHERTY EXPERIMENT
Lawrence Buentello

THE NEWLING
Paul Stansbury

THE SEVEN STAGES OF GRIEF
Diana Olney

TO THINE OWN SELF
Kelly S. Hossaini

WORM-SACKS AND DIRT-BACKS
Lee Clark Zumpe

CODED

Daniel M. Wilson

It's hot in here and the light blasting from the fluorescent strips above feels like a physical weight. The man opposite me raises the pen to his lips and taps it once against his front teeth before bringing it back to bear against the form he's filling out for me. He's left handed and the side of his ink-stained palm rubs against the fresh pen marks as he writes, smearing the words out into 3D. The pen is at his lips again, tapping. I follow a single bead of sweat as it springs into being at his hairline and wobbles down the side of his face.

'You're still feeling side effects?' he asks, eyes leaving the form for the first time.

I look down at my hands like I'm guilty before I can stop myself. I struggle not to vomit.

'No, none anymore."

My insides feel like pistons pumping congealed dog shit. I grip my hands tight together so they don't shake. I've been sick for what feels like forever, hereditary apparently, the only gift an absent father can give.

'Ok good. We've been experiencing issues with some subjects so we'll be glad to have you back again."

Is that smile supposed to be reassuring? I smile back. Our eyes meet and it feels all wrong; I'm looking through him, reading the clock on the wall behind his head, stuck, suspended in an interminable ten-fifteen P.M locked in his stare. He looks back down at the form.

Fuck me.

The doctor, my real doctor, said I probably don't have long left *"If I continue down this path".*

"Doc," I said. *"This ain't no path, it's a skydive and I jumped when I was thirteen".*

That was a while back now.

I put my hands in my jacket pockets and toy with the little plastic cat figure in there, spinning it quickly between my fingertips.

"So this is the last one?'

I try to control my voice but it squeezes out in a desperate little hiss. I don't think he reads my expression, to be honest I don't think he can. The barcode beneath his left eye twitches as he blinks slowly at me. It's shiny, catching the overhead light.

Who had he used to be? Has that left hand of his ended a life, or stolen something valuable enough that his life had been forfeit? That hand seems to me to be one that has squeezed a life to its ending, like toothpaste from a tube, irreversibly.

"Yes, this is the last. All things going well you won't need any more. We look forward to seeing you again very soon to study the results. We're all excited here."

He doesn't sound excited. Just repeating the script he's been given. One of many I'm sure, I doubt an asset of his value simply pushes pens in this small office all day. My eyes are drawn again to the mark on his cheek. Is my crime great enough to warrant a 'code?' Doubtful. Even deep in the throes of criminality as I am, sitting here in this chair and lying to this once-man's face. I wonder how much of him remains. It's never been made clear how much residual personality is left after a cauterization. Are there enough stalwart synapses left to propel about the skull what little remnants of personality are left behind? Sometimes it seems that way. Perhaps the attenuation of pathways allows only a tiny trickle through, and that's why occasional quirks express themself suddenly and randomly: a nervous tick here, a turn of phrase there. Each surfacing briefly from a grey, featureless psyche only to slip immediately back beneath the still waters of a dormant consciousness.

I look out the window to my right to avoid his eyes. We're high up on the thirteenth floor, it's raining and the city stretches away from me into the night. Far below a huge twisting intersection glitters white and red with the lights of vehicles and buildings like so many splintered teeth jut upwards into the distance. Huge neon signs dotted atop towers beam their messages out into the fog, luminescent colours smeared into the air like the ink on the form on the table. I feel trapped, like I'm in the vast mouth of a creature whose upper jaw hovers far above in the sky; I look up, waiting for a mirrored city to crash down through the smog above and crush us all. He hands me the dose. I can't take it here, something about liability. I tuck it into my coat pocket alongside the cat and leave.

I get in the elevator, some indistinguishable gunk is smeared across the buttons, I pull a piece of tissue from my pocket and press ground. Incongruously there's a doorman who watches me as I exit the elevator, he pushes open the door and holds it for me as I pass through. I step out the doors and descend the steps to the street.

Billboards prod me to buy stuff. Beautiful women clutching things I can't afford leer down at me in challenge. I feel vaguely emasculated. "Fuck off." I say, I whisper it under my breath.

The flashing billboards looming above reflect off the wet street, trapping me in a tunnel of light that funnels me onward like a human morsel down a neon digestive tract, my feet propelling me in spasmic peristalsis toward the bowels where I belong. As I walk further bright lights and feminine smiles give way to fugitive shadows that retreat ahead of me and gather in my wake. The ground is filthy here. There are no reflections underfoot, only a layer of greasy dirt. The faint bubble of distant music and conversation is replaced by harsher sounds: metal on metal, raised voices, screams. My fingers trace the contours of the cat in my pocket. A cat has nine lives, invincible basically, but what if it got stuck on one of them, paralysed, or trapped? And even if not, is its consciousness reset at each beginning or do they continue one into the next? A lifetime worth of suffering rolled over nine times. I shudder. It smells of death here, not the decay of living tissue but the stench of broken people. Nine deaths worth of stink at least.

I round a corner and the glowing lights of 'Jesse's Rest' spill down into the street. Saliva fizzes into my mouth and I'm suddenly aware that I desperately need a drink. I head inside.

Past the threshold it somehow seems darker in here than out on the street, the lights above sputtering an insipid, swampy light that falls onto the dingy interior and dingier patrons. A couple 'coded girls walk about the room. I take a seat and one approaches me.

"Can I get you a drink?" She leans forward catching my eye, winking. Programmed.

"Sure, I'll take a whiskey."

As she walks away I see a small bulge in her back pocket, her focus maybe. I look around the room. It's not an inspiring sight. It must be doing well for itself to have the 'coded girls here but it obviously wasn't being re-invested in the decor. One girl is up on stage gyrating in a way I'd probably find arousing if I didn't constantly feel like I was about to shit myself. Another is sitting in the corner on the far side of the bar. She's holding her focus, a little stuffed monkey, cupped close to her face as one hand mechanically strokes it from the top of its head down to the tip of its tail. She repeats the motion over and over as she stares into the black beads of its eyes.

I drink a couple more whiskeys.

A commotion breaks out on the far side of the room. One of the girls is screeching. I twist in my seat and crane over the booth wall to see. One of the dancers on stage is freaking out while the other 'coded girl backs away against the wall, her arms by her side, watching impassively. The screaming girl stops abruptly and begins shaking and tossing her head almost as if in a seizure, arms spasming out violently so that the cords of muscle in her forearms stand stark in her pale flesh. She stops suddenly, like a switch has been flipped. From here her eyes look bright and glassy, implacable and dangerous like twin headlights of an approaching train. Her head jerks down to look at one of the men sitting by the side of the stage. She walks forward, without urgency, and smashes his nose with her foot. He topples backwards with a cry and suddenly the barman is there. He grabs her, and whispering in her ear, marches her off the stage and out to the back. Jesse himself emerges from the same door and approaches the patron who's now on his feet holding red tissue to a bleeding nose. They converse quietly and also go into the back.

After a time the barman reappears and takes his place back behind the bar. My drink's out anyway so I head over. The guy's greasy looking. He suits this place.

"How's business?" I ask. The drunk's conversation starter.

"Not too bad, early yet." He says cagily. He holds a glass in one hand, polishing it with a grey cloth that may once have been white.

"What was that about?" I ask.

"We've lost her focus. Didn't realise she didn't have it on her 'til she booted that fella in the face!" He hacks out a laugh but seems to suddenly realise he probably shouldn't be telling me this.

I laugh along, "Risk you take here I s'pose. Hazard of the job, or hobby in his case." I nod towards the back door.

He finds this gratifyingly hilarious, or he just knows how to keep me drinking. I order another whiskey and take a stool by the bar but the conversation dries up immediately. I'm left staring into my glass and gripping my gut, digging into the soft flesh with gnarled fingers as if I can massage the rot away. I don't stay much longer. I pay my bill and leave the way I came. The bruised sky drops rain on me, the cold droplets cool on my flushed cheeks. I head home.

My house is ugly. The front door a mere suggestion, desperate that you believe it has the right to bar passage across its threshold. I unlock it with a shaky hand and step inside.

A tiny shadow spills out from the doorway of my room.

"Hello Lorelei, did you miss me?" I hold the little toy cat aloft so it catches the dismal light from the window.

"Tigs!" Lorelei rushes forward, snatching the cat, ignoring me as usual.

"I forgot to leave him to look after you, I hope you were okay without him." I say.

She looks okay, better than a week ago before the last treatment but worse than a couple days ago. I curse the time wasted, spent curled tight and spewing over the edge of the bed, unable to move.

We go outside into the yard. The rain on my skin distracts me from the clinging fetidness of the air. We sit on the bench with the spiralling wrought iron flowers and tigers that I dragged here a few months ago. I had hoped Lorelai would like it. She hadn't seemed to care one way or another, but occasionally I catch her out here, one hand dangling lazily over the arm-rest, her fingers tracing the patterns. She looks at me for the first time in a while.

"Can I fetch you a drink?"

"No sweetie, I'm not thirsty right now, thank you."

Sitting like this on the bench her bare legs dangle off the edge like skinny branches. She swings them absently and they're so thin it almost seems they're caught in the breeze. I reach into my pocket and pull out the dose. I press the nozzle to her thigh, next to the eight other marks. With an insectile hiss it's away, rushing through her veins faster than the poison in mine. I look down into her eyes and she up into mine. My knees shake. Her cheeks and the barcode beneath her eye catch the rain.

DREAMS HAVE CONSEQUENCES

Barry Vitcov

Butterfly

I once had a dream that I was a butterfly. Just once, never again. Although, I keep trying to repeat the dream without any success. I wasn't an ordinary butterfly like a common monarch or elegant swallowtail. In fact, I was a one-of-a-kind anti-chameleon butterfly, one moment blazing yellow, in another shimmering crimson, and sometimes deep violet. Anti-chameleon because I didn't change color to blend into my environment; rather, I burst into a dazzling, almost iridescent, display illuminating my presence and intending to attract attention. In spite of all that showmanship, I was not hunted by birds or cats or hunters with nets. My visibility seemed to make me more invisible, as someone to be avoided instead of engaged.

I would flit about without a care in the world. One moment I might be examining a flower to feast on sweet pollen and the next peering through a bedroom window looking for prurient delights. I used my lepidopteran order for natural, invasive and tasteless interests. I may have been a butterfly with normal butterfly behaviors, but I was also a human with normal primal inclinations.

The most adventurous part of my dream's journey was soaring into outer space. I was able to peer down and see earth in all its splendid and perilous condition. I simultaneously saw natural beauty, diversity and the horrific threats brought by human-made environmental abuses. It's fascinating how perspective becomes more meaningful and ambiguous from afar.

Dreams happen within milliseconds. They're like flashes of reality often without a satisfactory conclusion. Unless a nightmare over which we have no control, we want them to continue. I liked being an extravagant butterfly, free to gad about without consequence or responsibility.

Coastal Redwoods

Big Basin State Park is situated near enough to populated towns to make it readily accessible, yet isolated enough to make it a place to easily get lost. He enjoyed going off trail and wondering among ancient redwoods and tromping on the duff even though it was prohibited by park authorities. He felt entitled to finding his own way without directions or directives. One of the pleasures of Big Basin State Park is a trail the extends all the way to the Pacific Ocean. It's a fairly easy day hike and the trail is heavily traveled with passersby stopping to chat about what they've seen along the scenic route. He refuses to use the trail and has spent many hours trying to find an alternative trail to the sea.

It was a warm day in late July when he set out late in the afternoon seeking a new path. He believed that daylight saving time would provide enough time. He hadn't been off trail for very long when he spotted a banana slug. This one was an unusually bright yellow void of typical black spots. He thought it to be a purer form of the humongous slug. He used his iPhone to take several dozen pictures while admiring its shape and luminescent color. Suddenly he was overcome by an almost hypnotic state, losing track of time and direction. He came to his senses leaning up against a redwood stump just as dusk was settling in with an accompanying fog. His unease and disorientation increased as he became fully awake. He felt the incoming damp chill and, when he looked up, the sky was a haze and forest sounds had quieted.

He stood and tried to determine which direction to take back to the main trail. There were no footprints or other markers to help with navigation. He was smart enough to stay in place and not wander from what familiarity he had with his current situation. An inner calm replaced his initial fear and he remained against the tree stump for a few minutes before checking his iPhone and finding that he had a faint cell signal. He called his wife and explained his predicament. She asked for a landmark where he had left the main trail and urged him to stay in place while she contacted the park authorities. She was sure they would locate him soon and he agreed to wait and listen for help.

It seemed like hours had passed before he heard voices calling his name and flashlight beams dancing off tree trunks. He called back and within minutes three park rangers approached and led him back to the parking lot. Along the way, they chastised him for going off on his own and threatened him with future fines if he ever again walked into prohibited spaces.

Before driving home, he called his wife to assure her all was well. He sat in his car listening to Keith Jarrett play "Over the Rainbow" and thought about the languorous nature and freedom of that banana slug. The pictures on his iPhone captured all but its spirit.

Amazon Tunnel

They didn't realize how heavy dark could be until they were just a few feet inside the tunnel...four strangers, each in their own kayak, daisy-chained together by a thin wire, and led by a guide pulling them along with infrequent requests for them to paddle a few times to maintain constant flow along smooth waters with just a hint of resistant current. Their eyes began to adjust to never-experienced darkness and each tourist could see a kind of gray aura surrounding the person in front them. Their guide had made this trip several thousand times and knew each foot of the one-mile tunnel created by roots and vines twisted together forming a natural tunnel almost totally impenetrable by the humid light of the Amazonian rain forest. The natives referred to it as a Wonder of the World and accidentally discovered it when chasing a river dolphin. It didn't take long for Europeans to monetize this natural phenomenon into a popular tourist attraction.

He signed up for the tour on a whim. He was doing post-doctoral research on traditional medicines when he heard about the Amazon Tunnel and decided to spend a day and far more fortune than he could afford on the ride. He was seated in the last kayak. It was his choice; he wanted to observe everyone in front of him. The irony being that he could barely see past the woman in the boat just ahead and her blond hair turned out to be a distraction. He tried his best to look in any direction rather than straight ahead. The guides soft voice was almost inaudible, especially when the other three kayakers made soft noises just louder than their breaths. What he really sought was wonder, solitude and perhaps a unique vision he could hold for a lifetime.

The excursion lasted longer than he imagined. As they reached the end of the tunnel and hazy light began to emerge, their guide pointed them to notice the small pods hanging from above. Their guide explained that they were a magical fruit which grew in abundance in that part of the rainforest. The guide gave permission and encouragement to sample their special flavor.

Rudi reached up and plucked one about the size of a large grape. He bit into a tender skin with a slight crunch below the surface before a burst of menthol and dark chocolate overwhelmed his senses. As they emerged from the tunnel, color exploded and invaded his senses. He felt a hallucination of sensory experience unlike any other he had ever experienced. His pulse seemed to calm, which surprised him. The air seemed cool and fresh, not like the damp reality he had just left. He fixated on the woman's blond hair before him, as it seemed to glow from an inner light. He wondered what the future might really have in store.

The Dance

We were young and full of knowing. We met at the weekly Temple Beth Sholom dance, a place for young singles who didn't like bars or set-ups to meet and socialize. There was no expectation of religious belief or practice. That was reserved for Friday night or Saturday morning services, which neither of us as self-proclaimed secular Jews chose to attend. The temple's Hadassah affiliate had organized the Wednesday events for anyone who wanted to simply dance, enjoy the free refreshments...stale Costco cookies and overly sweet punch...and perhaps pick up one of the brochures addressing a pressing issue and leave a contribution. Jews are good at not tithing or passing a plate during religious services, but certainly not shy about asking for contributions to a worthy cause.

We had just signed the guest book and were mingling by the welcome table looking over the room filled with possibility when we bumped elbows.

"Excuse me," she was quick to say.

I looked at her and said, "I'm so sorry. I tend to unwittingly bump into people, walls, and other nearby objects."

She was quick to reply, "So, I'm just another object!"

"Again, I tend to figuratively and literally bump into things while, at the same time, putting my foot in my rather large mouth. How about we start over with a stale cookie and strawberry punch."

"Well, I hope it's not strawberry tonight. It was really overly sweet last week." She led the way to the refreshment table.

Rudy and Midge spent the evening in huddled conversation, in a corner of the room sitting on folding chairs without noticing how uncomfortable they should have been. They never noticed the other couples dancing and trying too hard to make a meaningful connection. Rudy became mesmerized by Midge's beauty. Her flowing blond hair, green eyes flecked with gold highlights, skin free of imperfections except for a tiny mole at the crown of her left cheek, and a figure he looked forward to holding when they would eventually dance.

When Rudy talked, Midge quietly eyed his dark, Eastern European handsomeness with bright, blue eyes, a comforting smile and a nose that appeared to have been broken one too many times.

"I tried boxing for a while, but my nose kept getting in the way, my footwork was never coordinated, and my punches landed mostly in thin air. I finally decided college was a safer choice."

He never stopped leaning forward with his elbows propped on his knees. They listened intently to one another and laughed at the same pauses; pauses that weren't caused by lack of things to say but rather by too much joyful similarity. "You mean your parents made you go to temple high school classes, too! And you were told you had to marry Jewish! Nothing less than four years of college and probably graduate school! I also hated my grandmother's kishkes."

They discovered common family histories; both having grandparents who immigrated from Russia; both having parents who made their parents proud; both having parents whom they found hard to please. They made dinner plans for the following Saturday.

Moshe's Deli had started as a small restaurant serving breakfast and lunch for several years before staying open for dinner with an expansion that more than doubled its seating capacity. Rudy and Midge sat across from each other munching on complementary slices of Moshe's dill pickles green tomatoes.

If this were a romantic story...and in fact it does turn out that way in the end, you might think that dinner led to more meaningful conversation and eventually physical intimacy. But that's not the way dinner progressed. After ordering their dinners, they found it difficult to begin a conversation, which led to increased uneasiness. They had arrived with elevated expectations but soon fell into a quiet malaise. After finishing dinner, they decided it would be best to return their respective homes.

"I was hoping that dinner would be a continuation of our time at the dance, and I'm disappointed. I guess it's best that we found that out early on," said Rudy.

"I agree," replied Midge.

For months, Rudy and Midge thought about their brief encounters. They had begun with surprise, pleasant conversation, uncovering of commonalities and hopefulness. They both felt they might have been experiencing dreams coming true, finding life partners without pretense or prearrangement.

It was many months before they decided to give the temple dance another try. Coincidentally, they both showed up on the same Wednesday. Midge came earlier and was standing by the refreshment table munching on a limp chocolate chip cookie and sipping mixed fruit punch when she saw Rudy enter and sign the guest book. When he looked in her direction, they both smiled with lips closed and straight-ahead looks. Rudy approached.

"How are the refreshments tonight?"

"The usual. Stale and sweet."

"I think that's what we became before giving ourselves a chance," said Rudy.

This time they ended up dancing together. Just slow dances because Rudy explained that he didn't have the rhythm for fast dances and warned Midge about the potential for stepping on her toes. She laughed and told him that she was well-prepared for klutzy dancers. As the evening ended, they agreed to try another date. He suggested a picnic in the city park.

"I'll put together a basket and we can rent a paddle boat and go over to Picnic Island."

"Food from Moshe's?" asked Midge.

"Absolutely."

Sunday began with a layer of dense fog and, by the time they arrived, the park was smothered with mist and the fresh scent of moisture and fir. Rudy assured Midge the fog would lift by the time they paddled over to the island. He rented a red paddle boat, loaded the basket behind the seats and handed the blanket, which he brought for them to picnic on, to Midge. They stepped into the boat, took their side-by-side seats and Midge wrapped herself in the blanket warding off more of the foggy chill. Picnic Island was in the middle of a man-made lake, which was no more than three or four feet at its deepest. It was about a quarter-mile paddle to the opposite side of the island where there was a small pier for picnickers to tie up their boats and disembark. The island was dense with fir, madrone and a few redwood trees. Scattered about were tables and benches and a number of clearings where a blanket could be spread out, and meals enjoyed. Rudy and Midge parked their paddle boat and noted that there were no other boats tied to the dock.

They found a clearing under a redwood tree and spread the blanket atop a bed of soft duff. Fortunately, they were warmly dressed and leaned up against the tree looking out at the lake which looked like a hazy mirage in the fog. The fog lingered but the chill seemed to be lifting.

"It's kind of spooky," said Midge. "I feel like we are looking through a kaleidoscope of crystalline shades of gray."

Rudy began pulling out a variety of Moshe's goodies: brisket sandwiches, egg and tuna salad sandwiches, dill pickles and pickled green tomatoes, three-bean salad, coconut macaroons and several bags of potato and corn chips. He also unpacked bottles of root beer and cream soda.

"So much food, Rudy. How did you know what I wanted?"

Rudy felt flushed. "I didn't ask. I'm so sorry. Well, this has really started off well."

"It's okay. I think you might be teachable. I actually like everything you've brought, so at least that's a good sign. And the sandwiches are all on rye bread, so that's another good sign."

They sat and ate a bit before Rudy said, "I once had a dream about being lost in a redwood forest and here we are sitting up against a redwood tree and I'm feeling lost for words."

"What I'm feeling at this very moment, Rudy, is a sense of comfort. Something tells me that we are in a magical place. That we were meant to be here at this very time. And I don't know why. I do love fog and how it colors the world with a sense of sameness and solitude which is very calming."

They ate and they talked. The words came easily with a deepening rapport. They discovered more than their family and their cultural pasts. They came to know shared values and aspirations. Their quirky senses of humor lightened every serious moment. They paused and they kissed.

The fog never fully lifted. While the day became comfortably warm, the fog pulled just above the lake while they ate strawberries and cheddar cheese before gathering up the basket and blanket and heading back to the paddle boat. Paddling back, they noticed how the fog reflected on the lake like a diaphanous ballet.

Midge asked Rudy to come back to her apartment where she offered wine and her bed. After making love, she turned on her side so that she could spoon into him. That's when he noticed a small, elegantly drawn black and yellow butterfly tattoo on her right shoulder.

I FEEL FINE

Sarah Archer

I saw in a TikTok that clenching a pen between your teeth tricks your brain into thinking that you're smiling and lifts your mood, so I'm sitting here at 3 AM, pen gripped between my teeth, waiting to not feel depressed, and all I really feel is that this is the saddest fucking thing I've ever done.

There's blunt moonlight tonight that cuts out each object in the living room from the black around it: the Toulouse-Lautrec poster on the wall. The pottery ashtray and crumpled paper towels and cracker wrappers on the pocked wood coffee table from my dead grandmother. The cheap wood molding, crooked, like this whole bland suburban apartment complex was slapped together too fast.

I just have to get through the night.

I could watch more TikToks, maybe. But you'll get three or four funny ones, and then they'll slip in something about police brutality, or a polar bear cub that got separated from its family on an ice floe cracked off by global warming. And I can't handle that shit tonight.

I could text a friend, but who wants to get a text at 3 AM? It's spooky. Besides, I don't want to be that needy person. *You up? I'm sad. Frowny face, frowny face.*

I could masturbate, but that sounds like a lot of work right now. Why is it so much harder for women to get off than men? It's like the finale of *Harry Potter and the Sorcerer's Stone*, where there are all these rooms and chambers you have to go through, and little hidden passages, and you have to solve a riddle, and you have to mix a potion, and find the right key, and fight off a monster, and then hours later, if you're lucky, if you survive, you MIGHT get the Stone. For men, it's like someone just dropped the Sorcerer's Stone on the ground outside.

So yeah. Another piece of bullshit I can't deal with right now.

I could eat. When was the last time I ate? But eating sounds like too much work too. Even the Lance crackers I left on the counter. I'd have to go to the kitchen. Unwrap them. Chew and swallow. You have to eat just to get the energy to eat. What a scam.

I can't sleep. What, you think I didn't try that one already?

I could just get all of this over with. It's not the first time I've thought about it—I've thought about it for years, imagining ways to do it. Like tying enough balloons to the couch that I float away into the sun. I like to dream up fanciful methods, instead of thinking about the bottle of pills I keep in the back of the medicine cabinet. But maybe I'm just too lazy and weak to get up the damn nerve. On any given day, it's always easier to stay. I really ought to stop futzing around and make a decision—*tomorrow*. Tomorrow, if I can make it there, I'll decide whether to stay or go. Maybe if something told me what to do. Like if I got some kind of sign.

There's a flash of light behind me that briefly illuminates the whole small living room. I hoist myself onto my knees on the sofa and turn to the window. There's a precise left-right-left jerking motion that I always have to do to open the janky old blinds. I peer out, leaning against the cushions. Outside I see a swath of the whole parking lot, the asphalt, and buildings of the sprawling complex, and tall black trees behind them, and a girl. She wanders in and out of the circumference of the greenish streetlight, no particular pattern, wearing a pale pink tank top and denim shorts, and no shoes. The cold of the night air chills my face through the glass.

I twist till my hair mashes the blinds, looking up and down the street. There's no one out there with her. Not that I can see. What the hell is she doing, by herself, at this time of night, in this weather, dressed like that?

I close the blinds and plop back down into my spot on the couch. There's a dent in one cushion from me always sitting on that side, though I'm the only one who lives here, and the right half of the dent dips deeper than the left. Jesus, even my spine is unbalanced. I spit the pen out into my hand and drop it on the table, cheek muscles aching. There's got to be some weed left in this bag, enough to get me through till the sun comes up. Daylight might yank me back from the edge of this sinkhole. But all my fingers find is papery crumbs. Shit.

I guess I ought to do something about the girl. But I don't want to. Maybe I'll just treat myself by pulling out my bottle of Elmer's glue, sliding a thin layer over my palms and fingers, waiting for it to dry, then peeling it off.

I turn back around and stare out the window again, prying the blinds apart with my fingers. The girl is gone. Good. I can just slip back into my thoughts. Regrets. Fears.

Here are several things I dread: Being trapped down an alley by a woman with a limp and long fingernails. North Korea nuking us. Getting high before the department's quarterly all-day meeting, but then having a bad trip and sitting there for hours, paranoid, confronted with a plate of danishes that've sprouted teeth. My childhood monster slithering up onto the mattress from under the bed. Dying of cancer. Sometimes I wish I had a terminal illness. That might give me a stronger desire to live.

Sometimes I wonder if the things I fear are actually things that will happen to me in the future and I'm not imagining them but remembering them, because time as we perceive it is an illusion.

The doorbell rings.

Fuck.

I slide my flip-flops on, though I have no intention of going outside. I swing the door open. At this time of night, it's probably someone here to steal my valuables or strangle me, watching my brave, bug-eyed struggle for life. Either way, I'll disappoint them.

But they're... me. I mean, it's the girl from the parking lot, in the pink tank top and shorts. But she's *me*. Or me the way I looked a decade ago, when I was thirteen. The frizzy brown hair I had before I started blowing it straight and dyed it deep purple. The skinny legs, with knees like knobby pine knots. The practiced arch of her eyebrows, a bad imitation of the sort of women in movies who wear black catsuits and punch men in the throat. I used to think I looked so cool.

"Why are you staring at me? Are you some kind of pervert?" she demands.

"If you're so worried about perverts, how come you showed up at a stranger's door at 3 AM?" It's got to be my eyes playing tricks, mixing the light and shadows on her face into a pattern I already know, or my brain fucking with me, tripped up by some combination of dopamine deprivation and the last fumes of an old high.

As she takes a step closer, the light shifts over her face and her features rearrange, like cherry icons on a slot machine falling into place. She doesn't look exactly like me after all. Her nose doesn't have the same twist to it, and there's a small mole in the center of her chin, like a cleft. I exhale, and it comes out shivery.

I was looking for a sign. This mysterious nocturnal visitor who looks like me is sign-ish. Though maybe signs are just bullshit.

"Do I know you?" She glances at the gold plastic 2C by the door. "Why did I come here?"

"I'm sorry, who are you? What do you want?"

She lets her eyes rove around before responding, as if her brain has a few other things to think about before me. Her bare arms hang loose by her sides, her legs cocked at a casual angle. The night air blows past her into my apartment and I'm clutching myself in my sweatshirt.

"I don't know."

"Are you here alone?" I lean forward enough to peer down the stairwell, squinting into the sparse bushes around the border of the building. There's probably someone hiding nearby filming this. Did they set me up with a mini doppelganger? That's awfully elaborate for a prank video. Maybe she's just bait to lure me to the door for the whole robbery/murder shebang. "Where are your parents?"

"I don't know," she says again.

"Well, where did you come from? Do you need a ride?"

"I don't know."

"This isn't funny, okay? Just tell me where you're supposed to be."

"I don't know where I'm supposed to be."

"For fu—for pete's sake." I move closer to the girl. There's that skepticism in the tilt of her eyes, but there's something else—something empty. Off. "Are you sick? Are you injured? Are you high?"

She giggles a little at that. "I don't think so."

"Aren't you at least cold?"

She looks down at her bare limbs, as if surprised to see them exposed. "I guess I am. So... what? Are you going to let me in?"

I glance out again, swiveling to look over the parking lot, the glittering expanse of asphalt. If this girl is acting, she's doing a damn good job. I guess I should be concerned about her. At least she'll occupy my time. Get me closer to morning, when I'll decide whether or not to take those pills, really. In fact, if time is an illusion, I've already decided.

I step back and let her through the door. "Why not?"

As she walks in, looking around, I switch on the living room light, shuffle off my flip-flops, and swipe the paper towel balls and cellophane wrappers into a pile on the coffee table. As if it matters—I'm bringing a stranger into my apartment at 3 AM. I should be worrying about getting shivved. She *is* a stranger. But every time I look at her face, I get creepy crawly. It's too familiar, but not. Like someone set a wet glass down on one of my old yearbook photos, and the paper got warped.

"So." I turn toward her, still wrapping my arms around myself, though I'm warming again. "Do you have anything in your pockets? A phone, a wallet?"

"What are you trying to do, rob me?"

"I let *you* into *my* apartment in the middle of the night. I'm trying to help. You don't have anything on you that would tell us who you are, or where you came from?"

She points her hips up one at a time as she digs her hands into her denim pockets, coming out empty. She shrugs. "Hey, you have the same color eyes as me."

"How did you get here? What's the last thing you remember?"

She twists a frizzy curl around her finger. "I don't know how I got here. It's like I don't remember anything." She giggles again, this time a little high-pitched, uneasy. "That's not normal, is it?" She catches sight of my lava lamp, sitting on the carpet. "Is that a lava lamp? Cool!" She bends before it and switches it on, gazing in awe as a glowing blue ball forms in the water. She just sits there, entranced, like a dog watching a ham on the counter.

"Did you hit your head?" I ask.

"How would I know that if I don't remember anything?"

"If this isn't a joke, you need to go to the hospital. I'm calling 911." I grab my phone from the coffee table, but she stands and stretches an arm out.

"No, don't call the police."

"Okay." I plunk the phone back down.

Her eyes narrow. "That's it? You're not going to insist on calling them?"

I shrug. "It's your life. It's your brain. If you don't want me to call, I won't."

"Don't you want to know *why* I don't want you to call the police?"

"I want to know why you came here, to my apartment."

"I told you, I don't know." She nods at the lava lamp. "Be careful. I heard they can break and leak everywhere. That thing is a time bomb."

I tug at the elbows of my sweatshirt. The presence of this girl is irritating. My throat aches from not crying. "Fine. If all you know is why you don't want me to call the police, tell me that."

The girl twists from side to side, like a little kid hiding something behind her back. "I–I do have a little memory. I think I was at a party earlier, and I think I was, you know, *drinking.*"

"How much?"

"I don't know, but I feel sort of weird and spacey." She giggles again. "Maybe I am high. Oh my God."

"You're up and walking, so you don't seem too bad."

"I just don't want to get arrested."

"The police are not going to arrest you."

"Well, I don't want my parents to find out."

"So you remember your parents? Call them."

"But I don't remember them. I just remember that I have them. At least, I assume I do. It's all, like–" She waves her hands around her head. "Woo-hoo! Spacey."

Whatever she took, I wish she'd brought some to share. "Well, then, I can't help you. You can't just stay here if you're not going to let me do anything."

Now she puts her hands on her hips, her skinny arms bowed out like wings. "You're not very nurturing, are you? A lost child shows up in the middle of the night, and you won't even help her."

"It's not my fault you're lost." It's all too weird, her coming here, looking like me, perky as a pansy, but not knowing her own name. Maybe she is the sign, but not a sign to off myself—a sign to keep living. The Ghost of Christmas Past or something. Is this some kind of *It's a Wonderful Life* situation? Jesus Christ.

"I'm thirsty. The least you could do is offer me something to drink."

"You're in awfully good shape for someone who just got drunk enough to forget her own name."

She draws herself up with a smile. "Thank you."

"I have tap water and I have tequila, so... tap water?"

"Tap water it is." She wanders around the room, totally comfortable. Picks up the TV remote and slaps it into her hand before replacing it on the table. Then she plops down onto the couch, on *my* side.

I shouldn't leave her unmonitored in my apartment for long, so I hurry into the kitchen, pushing my hair out of my eyes as I walk. I hate my purple hair now. I don't know what I'm going to do about it. The girl's voice reaches me from the living room. "I'm hungry too!" I take the packet of cheese crackers from the vinyl countertop and bring them out to her with the water.

She's on her knees on the couch, opening the blinds, deftly executing that left-right-left motion. "Hey!" I say as the blinds zip up.

She turns to face me. "What? I just want to look outside. Ooh." She climbs off the couch and takes the water and crackers, ripping open the cellophane and stuffing down a bite, an orange crumb falling to the floor. "I always ask my mom for these cracker sandwich things, but she says it's cheaper to get the store brand crackers and store brand peanut butter instead, so I have to make my own. These are better than the homemade ones. Well, they're worse, but they're better, you know? Hey, I remembered something about my mom! Still don't remember her name, though."

"How did you know how to open the blinds?"

She rolls her eyes and speaks through a mouthful of cracker. "I'm not *stupid*. It's not like I've forgotten how to do everything in life; I've just forgotten everything about me."

"But you knew how to open these specific blinds. You knew the trick."

"Huh." She looks back at the window. The streetlight buzzes outside, like television static. "I guess I did."

"Have you been here before? What've you been doing, casing the place?" Shit. I really do have to call the police. At least once they're here, they can take over. I step toward the coffee table and grab my phone before the girl can, but she's not even looking at it. She's staring into the dark doorway of the second bedroom. Throwing the wrapper down, she darts past me and into the bedroom.

"Hey!" I call out again.

"This was my room!" She flips on the light and blinks at the bright orange walls. Months ago, I started craving violent colors. I got the brightest paint I could find at the hardware store—kept trying to sell me some sort of russet, but no, I wanted safety orange. Now I hate it. I keep the light off; it takes too much energy to look at.

"What do you mean, your room?"

"My room, duh! I used to live here!" Her bushy hair fluffs over her shoulders as she looks around, nose crinkling. "Why is it so empty? And orange?"

I got a two-bedroom because I thought once I had an office, I would become a person who did office-centric things. Instead, the room is just empty, except for four cardboard pallets of Hormel chili and a gallon tub of Andes mints. The Costco membership was another brief, violent inspiration.

"This is the room where I keep chili," I say. "So you used to live here, in 2C?"

"That must be why I came back. And how I knew about the blinds. Yeah, this was my room! I wanted to paint it but my parents wouldn't let me. But I would never have painted it this color. No offense. And my parents' room was past the kitchen. You have another bedroom down there, right?"

"And now you and your parents live at?"

"Don't remember."

It was worth a try.

She pops off the lid of the Andes mint container and eats one. "Do you still have the baked potato button on the microwave, with the last *O* rubbed off? I always thought potatoes were called 'potats' when I was a kid. Potats, potats, potats."

"Come on, focus. Once you remember how to contact your parents, you can get out of here."

"Um, sorry, am I bugging you? I'm a *lost child.*"

Maybe it would be healthy for me to feel some concern for this young girl who's out alone with no memory. But it's asking all my strength to not just pull her outside by the skinny arm and leave her there, so I can sink back into the couch and mess around with my glue.

She runs her hand over a patch of wall near a corner, then suddenly stops. "There! My Pokémon sticker! You didn't bother to take it off before you painted. I traded Amy Ash a sandwich for that in second grade. I was hungry all day."

I slide my back down against the wall and sit, knees pointed up, head hanging. "Just keep remembering. Maybe you'll jog something loose."

"I used to brush my hair in here, and my mom would always get mad at me about leaving hairs on the carpet. And one time I tried exercising and I tripped and broke the window with my elbow, and I told the landlord it was a giant bird, so I had to go to the craft store and buy feathers to put on the carpet to try to prove it to him."

I lift my head. "That was me. I did that." A year ago. Fake eagle feathers. The landlord believed me. He's got the brain of a guinea pig.

"You did? That's funny. Maybe I don't remember it after all." She sits against the wall across from me, unfolds her gangly legs, and flops them out onto the floor, then presses her temples. "My head is starting to hurt."

"How can you remember something that I did?" Is this the sign?

"I don't know. Stop asking me questions. You think I want to be here? To not know who I am?"

"It kind of seems like you know who I am, if you know things that I've done alone in my apartment."

"Lady, I don't know anything about you!"

There's something not right here. But really, everything's not right, so I'm not going to think about it too hard.

She pulls her knees up into her arms. "Tell me about you while I wait to remember more."

Me—my least favorite subject. "Well, I live here. I work in the office of the comptroller."

"What do they do?" she asks, scrunching her nose.

"Nobody knows."

"Is that what you wanted to do when you were my age?"

"Definitely. My inner child delights every day." I tuck one leg under myself.

"Okay, so what do you do outside of work? Do you have a boyfriend?" A little smile curls at her lips.

I could tell her that there's a rotating cast of clowns I fuck when my self-loathing gets too acute, but I just say "No."

"Girlfriend?"

"No. I thought for a while I might be bi, but I'd just been watching *Amélie* a lot."

"No offense, but your life sounds pretty sad." She lies down, hands clasped over her stomach, staring at the ceiling.

I grimace. "You can't just say 'No offense' and then say something offensive."

"I'm just saying, you ought to be living life to the fullest."

"Thanks. I'll be sure to start doing that tomorrow." Maybe she is *It's a Wonderful Life*-ing me. If she's my guardian angel or something, where has she been this whole fucking time?

"Have you thought about going back to school?"

"You don't get to show up here at my apartment in the middle of the night and start counseling me. I'm helping you."

"You're not doing much to help." She wiggles her bare toes, looking at them. "How *did* I end up here? I can't have walked if I'm barefoot. But if somebody dropped me off, who would just leave me in a parking lot in the middle of the night? That's kind of scary, right?"

It is scary, and she's starting to actually sound scared, but it's hard for me to care. The ceiling light bouncing off the orange walls is giving me a headache. "You know, my job is actually really important and fulfilling," I tell her. "The comptroller is basically the kingpin of Branson. He pulls all the strings."

She looks at me, eyes large. "Like the Illuminati?"

"And I don't have a boyfriend, but I have a fiancé. He's a fashion photographer."

Now her eyes narrow again. "You're lying."

"It's more believable that I'm in the Illuminati than it is that I have a fiancé?"

"The Illuminati are real. Go on YouTube and search 'Rihanna lizard eyes.'"

"So you remember Rihanna but not your own name?"

"It's not my fault." She rubs her temples again. "I don't think it's my fault. What did I even do tonight? I don't like this."

I glance at my phone: 3:47. She was supposed to be my distraction, now I need a distraction from her. "Well, you got the tour. I obviously can't help and you won't let me call the police, so..."

"Are you seriously kicking me out?"

"We're not getting anywhere."

"Okay, I'm really going to try to remember. I'm going to remember everything that happened tonight and how I got here." The girl lies on her back, eyes closed, thin hands crossed over her chest, like she's on view at a wake. Sometimes I like to think about the ancient people that are probably mixed up down there in the ground beneath us, like it's just a basement unit in the building, full of other families. I think about the ribbons and boning knives and cat teeth that could be down there as part of the dirt. If time is an illusion, then the same teeth are in kittens and old cats and skeletons all at once. It doesn't seem like such a big deal to become part of that whole mess down there.

"Are you remembering?" I ask.

"Kind of." Her voice is smaller than before. "I remember the party. The house was blue. I don't know if it was the walls or the light—I just remember blue."

"Do you remember whose house it was? Name? Neighborhood?"

Her eyes cinch tighter shut. "I kind of remember vague faces... why can't I think? This is actually really bad, right?"

I wonder what could have happened to make this girl completely forget who she is. Maybe she was abducted by aliens, or had her memory wiped by a wizard or an FBI agent traveling back from the future.

"I'm sorry," she says. "I'm trying so hard." Her hands start to shake as she screws her face up. Her toes scrunch, turning the skin over the knuckles milk white.

Or maybe someone drugged and assaulted her at the party. Maybe it's the most predictable story in the book.

Remembering the past, or knowing what's going to happen in the future, is overrated anyway. If your brain is blocking something out, it's probably doing you a solid. Keeping the bad shit at bay.

"You can stop now," I tell her. "Stop trying."

She doesn't protest, just unscrews her face. "Thank you."

"You're welcome." Who am I to tell her to remember, or not remember? Like I know what to do. Maybe this small spurt of mercy was a bad thing, and she *should* remember. I've never been assaulted or anything. My life has been pretty nice.

She rolls over onto her side away from me, facing the wall. Her shoulder blades cut against the straps of her tank top, like contrails intersecting in the sky. Then those little hunched shoulders start to shake.

"Are you crying?"

"No." Her voice cracks on the word, and she buries her face in her hands. "I'm so scared," she sobs to the wall. "I just want to go home and I don't even know where that is. I don't know who I am. This is really messed up."

Something tugs in me, like my heart is snagged on a fish hook, being twitched down toward my stomach. If the drugs, or alcohol, or whatever is going on with her are wearing off, and she's starting to realize that she's stranded in a stranger's apartment in the middle of the night, without even her own name, she must be terrified. What if she never gets home? What if she never gets herself back? What if she does remember what happened earlier tonight, and it fucks her up for life? She looks so young like this, her string bean body tucked into fetal position, like she's waiting in a cupboard during hide and go seek. I've done shit-all to help; at least I could comfort her. I should go over and rub her bony shoulders, tell her she'll feel better tomorrow, tell her we'll figure it out.

But I might not even be here tomorrow myself. Maybe a self isn't such an important thing to lose, anyway. I stay seated against my wall, weighted to the carpet like there's sand in my ass. Just sit there and watch while she cries.

There's a popping sound from the next room. I walk out, the girl following, to see the lava lamp's glass shattered, a dark patch of fluid soaking into the carpet. "Whoa," she says, rubbing tears from her eyes with the heel of her hand.

I turn and look at her. She really does look like a younger me. It's fucking eerie. What did she say before about lava lamps breaking? That thing is a time bomb?

If this is the sign to kill myself, couldn't it have come without breaking my favorite lamp?

"Rhonda Wheeler," she says.

"You really are cracking up."

"No, I remembered! Rhonda Wheeler, that's my mom!"

"Rhonda Wheeler!" I open Facebook on my phone and search; the wet carpet can wait. I stop at the first middle-aged woman and thrust the phone in front of the girl's face. "Is that her?"

"Yes! Hi, Mom! It's coming back, I'm going to come back!"

I open a conversation and hand over the phone. "Tell her where you are. Go!"

She puts a finger to the phone, then stops. "Is she going to be mad at me?"

"Message the woman!"

She taps away on the phone for a while. This Boomer lady better have her notifications on. I want her to collect her child so I can flip over onto my stomach and lie face down on the carpet. The carpet is now wet and smelling like a biology experiment. I walk into the kitchen for paper towels.

Is there some part of me that wants to feel this way? Am I basically just watching myself in the mirror while depression fucks me from behind? Sometimes I wish I'd been abused as a child, physically, sexually, emotionally. That would provide a logical explanation for all the things that are wrong with me. It would give me someone to blame other than myself.

The girl is still looking at my phone when I return. "If your fiancé is a fashion photographer, why do your pictures suck? And why isn't he in any of them?"

"Give me that." I snatch the phone back. "Here, help me clean. You scrub. Don't touch that," I say as she goes for a shard of glass.

"FYI, I'm not leaving until my mom gets here. It's creepy outside," she calls, walking toward the kitchen with a clump of paper towels.

"If she's not here in half an hour, you still have to leave." I take a paper towel full of crunchy glass to the kitchen.

"It's freezing out!"

"That didn't bother you before."

"Am I going to have a hangover tomorrow?" She wraps her fingers around the kitchen doorframe, swinging herself in and out.

"If this is how you recover from getting blackout drunk, then I'm sure you can handle a hangover." I wish I was thirteen again, resilient as rubber.

My phone vibrates in my pocket. "It's Rhonda! Rhonda Wheeler is coming!"

"*Finally.*" The girl gives a dramatic swing and releases herself from the doorway. "So, uh, I kind of told her in the message that I was here visiting an old friend and we fell asleep watching a movie, and then her mom's car broke down so she couldn't take me home. I left out all the stuff about the party and the drinking and the memory loss. So you'll be cool, right? You won't tell my mom?"

I should definitely tell her mom. This girl ought to get checked out. "No, I won't tell."

She walks into the living room and I follow. She bends around the back of the couch, peering out the window to the parking lot.

I'd like to think I did a good deed here, helping this lost girl reunite with her family, but it's really more like a good deed dropped on my head and I bungled it. If this girl was a sign, or a test, or an omen, I've messed up whatever I was supposed to do. At least she'll be gone soon. In five years, she'll have forgotten all about this, and me. Whatever trace I left will have faded, if I left one at all.

Maybe tomorrow, I'll get my act together and kill myself, and this was the last chance I had to do something good, to give a person in need some sort of help or happiness. And I've done nothing for this girl. Nothing. I have to do something before she goes.

"Want to play with glue?" I ask her.

"Sniffing glue? Aren't you old enough to have better drugs?"

"Not to sniff it." I open the drawer of the TV cabinet and pull out my trusty bottle of Elmer's. I sit on the couch, and she sits beside me. "I just kind of put it on my hands, like this. Then when it dries, I peel it off."

"That's so gross." But she pours a quarter-sized glob onto her palm and smooths it around, following my lead.

"Not so much. It has to be super thin."

"And now you just wait for it to dry?"

"Yes. It only takes a couple minutes."

"I hope I've got more going on when I'm your age. No offense. Why do you do this?"

Because I can't mess it up. Because seeing my own fingerprints makes me feel more real. Because my fingerprints are a part of myself that I don't hate. "I don't know. It smells like elementary school."

The streetlight behind us keeps buzzing, its thin light spreading like water over the room. "Look, it's ready," I say, and start pulling. I always begin the same way, at the knob at the base of my thumb, and strip the widest, longest section I can off my palm. It stretches up from my skin like a cobweb anchored to a building, then breaks and comes off in one satisfying motion. I'll miss this if I never do it again. Or no, wait, I won't. I won't miss anything.

Is there any real chance that this is my last night alive? Or do I just talk a big talk, inside my head, to no one?

"Nice one," the girl says. She gets it. I'm glad.

She starts pulling off her own glue, and we add the peels to a joint pile on the coffee table, hers and mine jumbling together, like layers of old soil. They shrink down, curling in on themselves. Maybe my sign is in the peels. Maybe I'm supposed to look through them like tea leaves. Or maybe I'm not getting a sign at all.

"Why is there a cow on the label?" she asks.

"I think it's because glue is made from cows and horses," I say.

"Pretty sick branding move."

"Totally."

"I really wanted a horse when I was a kid," she says, picking a wisp from her pinky. "But my parents couldn't afford it, so I had this imaginary horse instead. Her name was Cloudy, and she was white and gray with a black stripe in her tail, and she would whinny and scuff the ground whenever I came up to her. And then one day I was in line at Subway with my dad and this teenage guy comes up to me, he had this weird shirt on, like an ostrich fighting a bald eagle or something, anyway, and he says 'Hey, I think you dropped this,' and he hands me a little toy horse. White and gray, with a black stripe in her tail. She came to me because I knew she would." Of course. To have such faith that fate operated on principle. "I loved Cloudy. I still have her."

The girl grins in a little-kid way, showing too much gum and not caring, as she gets a real satisfying piece of glue off and adds it to the pile. Hey, maybe it doesn't matter if she went through some shitty things tonight, if she went through good ones too. Me feeling like crap can't matter too much if other people are happy. It all kind of blends together in the end.

There's the sound of tires behind us, and we twist to look out the window. An old blue Honda zooms into the parking lot. The girl jumps up, flicking off a last shred from her palm onto the table. "They're here!" And just like that, her life is restored. She seems so happy to have it back.

"You really should go to the hospital," I tell her.

"Ughhh, I feel fine."

She's already at the door, turning the deadbolt. "Wait," I say.

"What?" She looks at me and I don't know what to say or do. I want to hold her like my body is her eggshell, to thank her, to reprimand her, to tell her to go to the hospital and get checked out, to tell her she's strong enough to take whatever comes next, to apologize that it was my door she ended up at tonight.

I pick up the mostly empty bottle of glue, shutting the cap and wiping the excess off the tip as I walk it over to her. "Here you go. Knock yourself out."

I expect her to say something snarky about my lame offering, but she just takes it with a smile. "Thanks. By the way, my name is Jessie. I remembered it like five minutes ago." And she's gone.

I head back to the couch and sink into my dip. The glue peels sit there, all wrinkly and dried up. I feel hollow, gutted with a spoon. It's funny to think about how all the time I've lived here, this girl was here before me, her spirit shadowing me through these rooms while I trim my toenails or boil water for macaroni and cheese. Maybe she's still here now; maybe everyone who's ever lived in this spot, even before and after this shitty apartment building's existence, is all here at once, dinosaurs and pilgrims and robots and stuff. But that's too much to think about right now. It hurts, like those vicious orange walls.

I get on my knees and look over the back of the couch in time to see Rhonda and Mr. Rhonda fly out of the car as their daughter walks toward them. They pull her in and huddle around her. Her dad kisses her forehead, and her mom sort of stretches her arms out, checking she's in one piece. She takes a handful of her daughter's hair and holds it, like she was so afraid to lose even that most transient part of her.

Now they're in the car, and the car slips into the distance, and there's no engine noise, no movement, just the deep darkness; it's gone.

The sky outside is going from black to gray, and at that moment the streetlight switches off with an angry zap, like a cat getting electrocuted. Suspended just above the spiky trees is a fragile ball of light. Maybe it's the sun, maybe it's the moon. Maybe both.

THE DARK GIFT

Daniel Loebl

Sam had a secret identity that only I was allowed to see. Abraxas was the god he worshiped in his one-room apartment. He had '365' tattooed on his right forearm. The number corresponded to the numerical value of the seven Greek letters that form the word Abraxas. I was the designated acolyte of his one-man cult. Sam's room was small and dark. He had painted the letters of the Greek version of Abraxas all over the walls in dripping red paint. On the wall behind his bed, he had painted a mural of Abraxas as an invincible wave crashing on the city, purifying it of its unworthy people. He had used a candle to burn black soot on the ceiling so the only bright area was where a single lightbulb hung like a remnant after a fire. Still, the place was a palace compared to my bedroom in my parent's house.

To start our worship, Sam and I danced in our underwear to Santana's Abraxas album. We drank beer while we danced, followed by some vodka, at which point, sweating and exhausted, we fell on his couch and watched old Hammer movies on television. Then, Sam would talk in his raspy low voice and I listened. He talked about the awful power of Abraxas. He promised that Abraxas would grant us power and success. Abraxas would remove our enemies; particularly Mr. Walker, our round, balding boss at the courier company. Our worship would guarantee us happiness and money and women.

On the morning of the layoffs, Sam and I arrived together at work after a long night of worship. Mr. Walker gathered the couriers into the cafeteria. Everyone wore the official orange uniform of the courier company with the cap that never kept us warm in the cold. Mr. Walker told us that he had to let go of some of us. He mentioned that the layoffs were caused by something to do with finance and accounting that we were not meant to understand. He would read the names of the employees to be laid off. Four security officers were ready to escort the laid off employees to the lockers and out of the building. Mr. Walker unfolded a long computer printout with many red marks visible through the paper. He started to read the last names of each person who was laid off. He had a droning, indifferent voice. He started on the As and made his way down alphabetically.

Sam bent towards me and hissed: "Pray to Abraxas." His words were garbled by sleep and vodka but I understood what he meant. Right away I told Abraxas, in my head, that I wanted to keep the job more than anything in the world. If he granted me this favor, I would dedicate myself to his worship forever.

A voiceless question filled my head like an ice-cold tide: Should I choose Sam instead? I knew what Abraxas wanted me to say. I glanced at Sam. He stood tall, muttering his prayers, certain of the protection of his god. I looked at the floor and shook my head. Choose me, Abraxas. I will be a better messenger. I swear it. I swear it, Abraxas!

To my surprise, it felt good to pledge my allegiance to the unpredictable god.

I heard a door slam shut. Startled, I realized that Mr. Walker had reached my last name on the list.

Mr. Walker stopped reading. He tilted his head as if he couldn't understand the words on the printout in front of him. The paper trembled in his hands. He frowned, hesitated, and cleared his throat. Then he called Sam's name. Sam turned to me, eyes wide open, ready to scream his frustration. He raised his hands to my neck. Security guards escorted him to the lockers to take his uniform and then walked him out of the building. I only saw Sam's back as he twisted against the hands that held his arms in place. No one noticed the grin on my face.

Sam had been abandoned by his god and the loneliness was unbearable. He didn't handle it well. He pleaded with me for a visit of any sort. Let's go to the movies. Let's get a sandwich. Let's hang out on my couch. He called upon our friendship. He said I owed it to him to visit. I didn't reply to Sam's texts or voice messages. I blocked his number after hearing him crying in many drunken, helpless calls. Three months passed in silence between us. I was surprised to feel an urge to stop by his building to see how he was. Maybe I felt pity. Maybe I felt I owed him. I can't pin the reason I walked up the stairs to Sam's apartment.

An angry man in a blue suit stood outside of Sam's apartment. His face was round and red. He was yelling at two young men to paint the walls beige and the ceiling white.

"You can't count on people," he told me and pointed at Sam's apartment behind him with a puffy thumb. "Look at the mess I have to deal with. And no rent paid for three whole months."

Suddenly, looking puzzled, he tilted his head. "What do you want here, anyway?"

An ice-cold wind filled my head. I've taken Sam, Abraxas said. Prepare yourself for my worship.

I didn't answer the man in the blue suit. I walked past him back to the street.

From that day on, things started to change at work. The employees who Mr. Walker kept got a raise as a thank you for sticking with the company. Mr. Walker himself was fired. He was too expensive to keep. He was replaced by a younger man who expected couriers to disappear from the job without warning. He took pride in considering his employees as interchangeable. He let us get away with goofing off on the job as much as we wanted as long as we respected him and covered for each other when the higher ups came to visit so he could keep his place in the hierarchy.

Now, I'm the king of the couriers. Everyone likes to party with me. My colleagues marvel at my big new apartment. They marvel at the blacklight paintings on my walls, at the undulating black and red lines on the ceilings. They can see that I live better than they do. They wonder what my secret is. Are you selling drugs on the side? Is your family rich? I laugh and I tell them the secret is my philosophy of life. They ask me what it is and I tell them: It's a little worship I do every day. They want to try it out to see if it will make their lives be like mine.

And so we start. We dance to Santana. We drink vodka and beer. As a game, I have them pledge drunken allegiance to Abraxas, whose face fills one of the walls in the living room. I tell them that I owe it all to him. They laugh and think I'm peculiar. They pledge allegiance anyway, half believing, half hoping to believe in a power that can change their lives in an instant.

Abraxas can tell who believes and who doesn't. He tells me who to pursue and slowly, very slowly, helps me convince them of the rightfulness of his path.

Sam never understood Abraxas' needs. I do. I am the prophet of Abraxas, the one who feeds the faithful's flesh to Abraxas so he can live forever. That's my task. I'll pursue it with full dedication and love until he calls on me to meet him in person.

BEYOND THE BLACK CURTAIN: AWAKENING

Wayne Kyle Spitzer

I | Awakening

She awakened with a rush, drawing in air which smelled like ammonia and pain, and found herself lying on the floor of the gondola while Dravidian crouched over her and Milkweed—Milkweed! She lived!—purred against her ear. The gondola's lanterns had been extinguished so that they floated in near blackness.

"My lungs burn," she managed, reaching up to pet Milkweed and realizing suddenly that both her wrists were now free of shackles.

"It's the smelling salts," said Dravidian. "It will dissipate quickly. How do you feel otherwise?"

"I feel—I dreamed of a white fountain." She looked into his eyes. "You were there with me ..." She drew her hand away from Milkweed and rubbed the ignudi dust (so prized for its qualities as an aphrodisiac) between her fingers. "So were you, Milkweed, it seems."

"There's been an attack," said Dravidian—then paused, holding a black gloved hand to his temple.

Shekalane heard a jumble of garbled voices emanating from his mask's circuitry.

"At least one ferryman and his charge have been killed," he said, "and power stations throughout Ursathrax have been sabotaged."

"A ferryman killed? But how ...?"

"I don't know. Early reports indicate the terrorist Valdus is using a new weapon—one capable of penetrating shields." He stood abruptly. "I must get us underway. So long as we drift we are particularly vulnerable."

"This weapon ..." She sat up on her elbows. "Is that what caused the white light?"

"Yes," he said, and mounted his dais. "As well as the shock wave that rendered you unconscious. I, too, lost consciousness briefly." His fingers danced across the control pad as he appeared to check readings. "I'm redirecting all power to the port and starboard shields. But with weaponized energy of that magnitude ...."

Shekalane thought of the ring and sat up the rest of the way, her senses rapidly returning. "Where are we? And how long was I out?"

He took up his oar and placed it in the forcola. "About an hour. You stirred once in response to smelling salts—you must not remember—then fell into a deep sleep." He turned his mask to face her as he began rowing. "Our charges often haven't slept for days prior to the Sacrificium—I estimated you needed the rest. As for where we are at, we are approaching the Archon Narrows."

She looked at the green ring. *Activate it by pressing the emerald when you approach the Stygian Flowstones ...*

"Dravidian, I—I've always wanted to see the Stygian Flowstones. And now—with our fates in the balance—I wish to see them more than ever. Will we be passing them soon?"

"I am sorry, Shekalane. But we passed them while you slumbered. Had I known of your wish I would have awakened you and rowed us close. It is a custom among us, some of us, to grant such last wishes when we can."

The magnanimousness of such a custom struck her, and she looked at Dravidian—pushing and drawing on his oar, harder even than he had before they'd gained the middle of the river, and realized he was doing it for them. For her. To protect her.

The ferryman is already dead.

She could not disregard that part of the note. And yet— was she herself not, in a sense, "already dead," if the near certainty of being forced into sexual slavery didn't drive her to act?

There is no choice, Shekalane. You must activate the ring.

But her conviction swayed like a tree in the wind. How could she possibly do that now that she knew her jailor as a man and not a monster? Now that she knew him as a man of uncommon depth for whom she felt—did she dare even think it?—a *stirring?*

Again the pendulum swung. It was all well and good to have met a kindred spirit on the way, but he himself had said they wouldn't see each other again after her deliverance. Certainly she had to consider her own survival first—wasn't it at least possible that Valdus would spare him if she were to ask?

A new weapon. One capable of penetrating shields.
The terrorist Valdus.

No. No, she was being a fool if she thought Valdus would spare an enemy, much less a ferryman same as Asmodeus, for whom his hatred was complete. Nor could there be any warning if such a weapon were being used; indeed, they could be stricken at any instant, and he (Valdus) had already shown his willingness to risk innocent life.

Again she looked at Dravidian, at the strangely earnest living-dead man intent upon his rowing, as well as the weapon hung heavy at his hip, glinting, and the answer came to her with such sudden clarity that she was amazed she hadn't seen it before.

Activating the ring was their best and possibly only chance for survival. Even Valdus would not risk the life of his own betrothed in order to simply kill another ferryman, she was sure. And thus he would be forced to approach them and penetrate the shields slowly, which would allow her an opportunity to negotiate or at very least give Dravidian a chance to defend himself.

She fingered the ring gently. *Forgive me, Dravidian.*

She had just started to press when Sthulhu came cawing back out of the gloom—urgently, frantically (causing Milkweed to dart away yet again), and alighted on Dravidian's upraised arm.

II | Crucible

"What is it, Sthulhu? Speak."

"Enemies," said the raven. "Port and stern. Many men, heavily armed, *awk!*"

Dravidian began to reply when a great sound tore the night—a sound so lumbersome and ultimately shrill that it could only be iron crying out in distress. It came at once from left and right, and was followed by what sounded like chains rattling—but hundreds of chains, *thousands* of chains!—as water gurgled and dripped, after which a third sound, a sound which clanked and creaked and ratcheted faster and faster, grew prominently amidst the cacophony.

Shekalane saw light from the *orbis lunae* glint metallically in the blackness ahead of them. Dravidian must have seen it too, for he triggered the bow spotlight, which shown whitely from the blade-like ferro and revealed an enormous blasting net—impossible—rising from the blackened waters. No, not one blasting net, Shekalane realized, but many, all conjoined so that they spanned the entire width of the Narrows!

"Enemy closing off the port bow," said Sthulhu, who had leapt from Dravidian's arm to the top of the ferro and trained his red beam on the shore.

Dravidian activated the port spotlight and Shekalane saw longboats with many oars approaching rapidly; she counted five, maybe six, spearheaded by a green lead boat—at the bow of which crouched a man in a hooded cloak of the same color.

She leapt to her feet almost instinctively. "It is Valdus!" she cried.

A bright light caught the corner of her eye and she looked behind them; Dravidian had activated the stern spotlight so that yet more boats were visible—a mid-sized vessel with a small cabin and two additional longboats—which were closing rapidly. All of the ships both port and stern bristled with men and arms.

"Dravidian—what do we do?"

He commanded: "Sthulhu, quickly, while they are blinded by the spotlights, locate the next *vetitum portas*. It should be near."

She saw the raven's beam swing in the dark—then lock onto something. "Exactly one nautical mile," he said. "As the crow flies, *awk!*"

They were again engulfed in blackness as Dravidian killed the lights. "Sthulhu, distract them," he ordered—and she heard the bird's wings beat furiously into the night. To her he said: "The key around my neck is to access the processing terminal at the end of Ursathrax. But it will also open the *vetitum portas*—the gateways to the Forbidden Channels—although we are forbidden to do so except in the direst emergency. You may have noticed there is no riverbank on our starboard side in this region, therefore there is nowhere else to go. I will angle us for the doorway but I can't promise I will judge the distance correctly or that I will be able to out-row our attackers. I—I have heard the rebels have begun capturing women and children for use as human shields. I will do my best, Shekalane. You are free to help me if you wish; there is an extra oar attached to the gunwale directly behind you. The decision, of course, is yours."

She watched as he began rowing with powerful strokes, her vision having grown somewhat accustomed to the dark, rubbing her wrist as she did so, then turned and looked at the oar fastened to the gunwale.

"It is the Hour of a Thousand Paths, ferryman!" Valdus shouted as he and his men approached. "The hour in which anything is possible! Our killing of your brother is proof of that! Prepare to be boarded and to leave both the girl and this world behind. Long live the revolution!"

She peered into the night and could just make out his form amidst the boats, her handsome and dangerous former lover come to rescue her, her darkling Prince of the Revolution who in the end had not forgotten her. They were too close now; the ferryman—*Dravidian*—as skilled and powerful as he was, would never outrun them. Her mind seemed suddenly full of nonsense now that the experience had ended and the outcome seemed certain, as though she had regressed to an earlier, infant state. It would be a short, brutal life with him—with Valdus—but it would be free, nor would it be without passion, at least when he wasn't tilting at his windmill or chasing his whale, and it would change the world forever so that no one need fear the ferryman or labor beneath the Lucitor's yoke ever again.

She looked forward at Dravidian, who was also a mere shape in the night, and her heart pounded as she watched him draw upon his oar. *Beautiful, undead stranger, who bid you welcome into my heart and made me feel for you almost as a lover? Will you not still deliver me to your Lucitor if you survive? Will you not use your key again to open the gates of hell at the processing terminal only to row away from me forever with your humane, dreaming eyes and your thoughts and quotes of Montair? Who are you to me, ferryman, and who am I to you? Is it selfish of me to want to live even if that means you will* surely die? And are you not doing the same? Life is selfish, only a fool believes otherwise; passion is selfish, and above all, love is selfish!*

She looked toward Valdus and saw that he was close enough to make eye contact with, and she did so lingeringly, seeing in his face something she had never seen there before, something eager and pure and almost innocent; he was as a child to her in that instant, and yet he was also as a stranger, like something from another life altogether, whereas Dravidian somehow shared her time and space and interiority, had done so, somehow, even before she had met him, and as she turned away from them both to ponder the extra oar she wondered how the word "love" had even come into her mind.

You try so hard just to make do and to get by, she thought, *You try and you try and you try. And some days, you succeed! But then comes a black coin to first your husband's palm and then your son's, and finally your own, and everything you thought you knew is suddenly up for reinterpretation. Then comes a lover who is obsessed for all the right reasons but still obsessed, then comes war and rebellion and the Hour of a Thousand Paths in which anything and everything is possible. And then, just when you think you can peaceably say goodbye to it all, when the numbness finally becomes libation instead of pain, then ...*

Comes a ferryman.

And it was at that moment and none before that she realized precisely what she had to do.

III | Pursuit

By the time Shekalane unfastened the spare oar (which was surprisingly heavy and more than twice her height) and began to paddle desperately, the rebels' boats had closed to within a hundred feet and the glinting tips of their weapons could be clearly delineated, even in the dim light of the distant *orbis lunae.* Nor did her initial efforts, performed under such duress, achieve anything but to disrupt their course.

"No, Shekalane," said Dravidian, seeming inhumanly calm given the circumstances, "you must row on the other side. Place it in the forcola—the rowlock. And mind your balance."

She did as instructed, placing the oar's shaft at random amidst the forcola's grooves and starting to pull and draw on it furiously—but the pole kept slipping, forcing her to spend most her time and energy trying to replace it in the rowlock, prompting Dravidian to shout, "Easy does it, Shekalane! Subtlety, not brute force! Hold the oar palm-down and don't squeeze, and follow it with your body."

Again, she did as instructed, and to her surprise, her movements began evening out and she became more surefooted.

"That's it," said Dravidian. "Row from your stomach. Think of it as walking on the water."

She did so, concentrating furiously, minding her footing, telling herself to breathe. She was doing something right; their speed had clearly increased. She spared a glance over her shoulder and saw Sthulhu hovering erratically in front of first one boat then the other, aiming his ruby-red beam in the men's eyes, causing the ships to slow and to lose direction.

"Mind your oar, Shekalane. We are almost there."

And suddenly they *were* there, and the gondola's steel ferro had served its purpose by clanging against the iron door and preventing any damage to the shell of the ship. Shekalane turned to see Dravidian whip the chain of the great arrow-headed key over his head and insert the instrument into an equally great keyhole, which glowed blood red inside and activated a green light on the console—which caused the leviathan door to shudder and groan and to begin rising.

"Dravidian!" Shekalane barked, seeing how close Valdus and his men were, and also seeing Sthulhu dive upon Valdus' face in a ferocious attack, which forced her former lover to grapple with the beast and to lose his focus, however temporarily.

Dravidian saw it too, and called harshly, "Sthulhu! Come!"

He steered them into the passage even as the great door with its widely-grated bottom began closing again, and the last she saw of Valdus after he had pressed the raven to the floor and slammed an inverted crate over him was the man standing suddenly and looking at her with an expression of complete and utter betrayal.

THE DOHERTY EXPERIMENT

Lawrence Buentello

When Dr. Thomas Doherty closed his office door for the last time and drove away to his summer house in the country, only those in the College of Social Sciences marked his departure with concern; the loss of any tenured faculty member might raise interest in a smaller university, but in one as large as ours such events weren't uncommon.

His abrupt exodus, however, was of primary concern to those for whom he served as doctoral thesis advisor, and as I was one of those falling under this aegis, I found his abandonment of his position as Senior Professor of Sociology more than concerning. The question of *why* he'd left his office for the duration remained the business of our Human Resources office. But when I inquired with the chairperson of the department as to the disposition of *my* research, closely associated, as it was, to Dr. Doherty's highly publicized research, she soberly informed me I would soon find myself under the supervision of a new doctoral advisor, that Thomas Doherty had resigned his position, effective immediately, and wished no further contact with anyone from the university.

This state of affairs seemed completely incongruent with the man I'd come to know. I'd studied under him closely while earning my graduate degree and had maneuvered through significant obstacles to become one of his research assistants while conducting my own research for the drafting of my dissertation. Doherty at no time seemed to me to be anything but an enthusiastic scholar, exuberant in his studies, and determined to ensure his name resided in some high regard within his field. A tall man in his early fifties, the hair on his slightly balding head still coal black, his blue eyes sharp and piercing, Doherty appeared vital and self-possessed, the author of many highly regarded papers on the prediction of social trends, and a natural communicator who never missed an opportunity to dominate a conversation.

My own work, the creation of social models precisely mapping the evolution of historical cultures, dovetailed perfectly into his greater study, the designing of nested algorithms which would accurately predict the future presentation of specific and general social systems. He'd been compiling an extensive computer algorithm for years for just this purpose, and, using my own models, those of two other graduate assistants, and his own extensive research, had finally completed the massive data-rich programming designed to provide, in his own words, *an accurate depiction of the future evolution of the human species.*

The day after Doherty ostensibly processed all this information through the university's array of supercomputers to obtain his final results, he quit his office and vanished into the countryside.

I and those others with a vested interest in his experiment's results would have been alerted to this circumstance earlier if

Dr. Doherty hadn't been so secretive in his actions. One of his less than admirable traits was a distinct distrust of his fellow researchers, who he considered completely unreliable. Perhaps he'd experienced negative interactions in his youth, or had his research compromised or even stolen, but his paranoia proved insoluble to those of us attempting to invest his insights into our own work. He never revealed the extent of his programming to those of us working to provide him with useful data, deciding to partition his interactions and forbidding us to consult with one another. The results of his labors, he announced, would be presented once he'd produced an animation of the outcome, an 'accurate vision of the future' played before the eyes of the world.

But before Doherty so abruptly left the university he first encrypted all his computer files and shredded his papers into confetti.

I would have had an easier time reassembling his confetti: aside from being a prominent sociologist, Doherty also held a graduate degree in computer sciences. Early in his career, he'd consulted on encryption techniques for the NSA. Without his intervention, no one would ever peruse the files he'd produced from his experiment.

But I couldn't so blithely dismiss Doherty's inexplicable collapse, because the efficacy of my own research depended on the usability of the data sets I'd provided him for use in his experiment. I had to know Doherty's disposition, and, more importantly, for the sake of my curiosity I had to know the outcome of his experiment.

My official inquiries were met with complete disinterest—if Doherty had left the university for personal reasons then those reasons were none of my business; if he'd left for medical reasons then those reasons were protected from curious eyes by abiding health laws. In other words, if he'd wanted me to know he would have told me, and since he didn't I would just have to wait until I spoke to my new advisor.

But if official inquiries were useless, perhaps unofficial inquiries might prove more useful.

I knew that I and two other doctoral students compiled the social grouping data Doherty was to use in his experiment—I created the massive data set comprising human history from prehistory to the Industrial Age; Curtis compiled the data set from the Industrial Age to the Atomic Age; and Raghavan compiled the data set from the Atomic to Contemporary. These immense sets of information were the foundation for Doherty's experiment, which, if successful, would accurately predict future trends based on mapped evolutionary patterns as demonstrated by our data sets.

The process of this evolutionary progression lay in Doherty's secretive computer program.

Since neither Curtis, Raghavan, or I knew any of the details of the computer system Doherty intended to use, I sought out the last doctoral student on his team, Allison Gayheart, though I really had little interaction with her previous to Doherty's disappearance.

Doherty's desire to keep the component parts of his experiment from interested eyes meant that none of his assistants knew much about the totality of his project. And he discouraged us from talking amongst ourselves, using a subtle threat of dismissal as his weapon of enforcement.

I found Allison in one of the smaller computer labs usually reserved for graduate students for compiling their coding projects over long hours in relative quiet. She wasn't in the process of refining code that morning, but was actually drafting her request to be transferred to the doctoral advisor of her choosing. Such requests were, at best, not much better than investing in a wish.

"I never wanted to be part of Doherty's department," she told me as she moved her black hair from her shoulders. Her small face, made smaller by large black glasses, held her disdain for the entire situation like a pall. "No one else would pick me up at the time. But he needed someone to write your sets into executable subroutines and I needed an advisor. I had no idea I'd be wasting a year writing code for a lunatic."

Of course I didn't believe Doherty was a lunatic. Paranoid, yes, and a narcissist, but not crazy. He didn't speak to me about the details of his experiment, except to say that his results would revolutionize his field, but he did wax eloquently of everything he'd sacrificed to accomplish his goals. Unmarried, solitary, insular, he'd dedicated his life to his studies and, because he had no other precious commodities in his purview, he viewed his approach to life as sacrosanct, his justification for his eccentricities being the brilliance of his future accomplishments.

Doherty was certainly a prima donna, but he wasn't mentally ill, or, at least, I'd never perceived him as affected—except for his sudden departure from an academic lifestyle he'd pronounced as sacrosanct.

"Do you have any idea of his protocol?" I asked her. "Or any notion as to why he left the university after running his precious experiment?"

She smiled. "You want to know because he left you high and dry, too."

"He left four of us high and dry, so, yes, I'd like to know *why*. More than that, I'd like to know if the results of his experiment can be salvaged so I can complete my damned dissertation."

"That's not going to happen without Dr. Doherty's blessing. The first thing I did when I found out he'd left the university was to go to the Prime Labs where he compiled his program. But his work was gone, tied up in a double layer of encryption I couldn't even begin to unlock. It's the modern equivalent of burning all your papers. Only *he* can unlock the encryption, but he told the lab coordinator he'd never see him again and to just write over the memory."

"*Has* he written over the files?"

"Not yet. I told him to keep it partitioned for a while, just in case Doherty changes his mind."

"Do you think he *will* change his mind?"

"No."

I shook my head, wondering how she could be so certain. People changed their minds all the time—if Doherty's experiment didn't produce the results he wanted, he could always try again with different data, couldn't he?

But it wasn't so easy, Allison explained. The massive data sets Curtis, Raghavan, and I designed were already run for efficacy. In other words, Doherty had created algorithms for subroutines that verified, according to his master program, that given the data parameters of the information, the evolutionary development of human societies progressed precisely as they had historically.

This meant that, using the same data sets and evolutionary parameters, Doherty's 'master program' could in theory foresee trends based on social and biological factors to precisely predict the future profile of the human species.

"He nested his algorithms," Allison said, rocking slightly in her chair. "It's quite brilliant, actually. One algorithm would produce an evolutionary result that would feed into a multitude of other algorithms that would produce evolutionary results that would then become the data sets for the nest algorithm. The final result would be an overview of the future evolutionary pattern."

"He told you this?"

"Not in so many words. I extrapolated most of it from the way he had me structure the architecture for your data sets."

Doherty once told me, perhaps in a weak moment of hubris, that he intended to produce an animated video of humanity's future world that would win him a Nobel Prize. In fact, his methodology would send Probability Theory into obsolescence.

"Do you think his experiment succeeded?" I asked. Suddenly the room felt claustrophobic.

She smiled grimly. "You'd have to ask him."

I suppose I would. "Allison, you wouldn't happen to know the location of Doherty's house in the country, would you?"

"Confronting Doherty, as much as I'd like to myself, might get you into a lot of trouble, Daniel."

"What he did to us is unconscionable." I actually believed this, too. "He should have had more academic integrity. I want to know *why*. Don't you think we deserve an answer?"

"I suspect any answer we'd get wouldn't satisfy us much. I worked with that egomaniac for nearly a year. His experiment busted out, so did his ego. He's a lost cause."

"I'd still like to know. Do you have his address?"

"It shouldn't be difficult to acquire," she said after a moment, her voice assuming a false air of authority. "If it's not on the web, I can just hack into Human Resources. Their information isn't encrypted."

I smiled at her, impressed by her skills. "I hope HR doesn't have any of my credit numbers on file."

"Would it matter? You're a doctoral student like me, and probably just as broke as I am."

Allison Gayheart passed along Doherty's country address without elaborating on her method for acquiring it.

The following day, and with nothing to do even though the semester hadn't yet concluded, I borrowed my roommate's truck and drove twenty-five miles out of the city in search of Doherty.

I found myself surprised by how quickly the trappings of concrete civilization metamorphosed into rural farmland and dusty county roads. If it was Doherty's desire to find himself isolated from the grinding machine of academia from time to time, if only to develop his concepts in a quiet location, he'd chosen wisely. After twenty minutes I found the route marker on the unpaved road and turned the truck toward Doherty's house.

His residence wasn't meant as a farm house, obviously, since the small white frame house in the middle of nowhere lay surrounded by rustling fields of untamed wild grasses. A swath of pruned vegetation extended from the foundation in a twenty meter circle, giving the house the appearance of a civilized island in a sea of wilderness.

I parked my roommate's Ford by Doherty's luxury sedan and walked up the steps of the porch, noting the cleanliness and fine condition of the residence, undoubtedly a symptom of the man's high regard for himself and those things in his life that announced it to the world.

At first, no one responded to my repeated knocking. With nowhere to go in the immediate area, and his car suggesting his presence, I knew he had to be inside. After a moment, I caught his appearance at one of the front windows in the corner of my eye—his wide forehead shone with the sunlight, and his blue eyes watched me as if he'd found a ghost on his front porch.

I called his name, but he just stood in the window like an idol.

Finally, after resuming my assault on his front door, he moved slowly from the window, the curtains swaying into place. A moment later the lock turned, the door opened, and Dr. Thomas Doherty stood staring at me from the shadows of his living room.

Gathering my resolve, which was quickly fading under the circumstances, I said, "Dr. Doherty, I came to speak to you."

His gaze flashed at the truck by his sedan, then back to me. "Go home, Daniel."

"I'm not going home until I speak to you. Listen, I *have* to speak to you about our research. About your experiment."

"I have nothing to say." His voice, normally full of the enthusiasm of his profession, sounded flat in the air, lifeless. "The experiment is over. And you must know by now that I've left the university. Nothing remains to be said."

"You owe us an explanation."

"Who?"

"The four graduate assistants who spent the better part of a year collating data for you. Don't you remember? The data sets we were going to use to prove our dissertations on historical social development?"

"You'll get another advisor."

"My doctoral dissertation is tied to *you*, Dr. Doherty. *And* your experiment. A pile of data doesn't prove anything. Your computer program was supposed to prove its value. We need the results of your experiment."

Now Doherty, disheveled in a denim work shirt and chinos, in stark contrast to the tailored suits he usually wore, laughed deeply, his face, though, reflecting little humor. "All my life," he said, his laughter subsiding. "All my life. What for?"

He turned away from the door, leaving it open on me and the world.

Uncertain, but determined, I followed him into the shadows of the room. The room lay furnished for comfort and elegance, and for entertaining, I imagined, tenured professors and colleagues vital to the maintenance of an academic reputation. But all the country styling of the room, the paisley chairs, the latticed wallpaper, the finely carved tables were only decorations of leisure, not the artifacts of an actual life spent living in the country. Why Doherty had retreated to such a place I had no idea.

Doherty sat in one of the chairs, rumpled, common. The small table at his right hand held a nearly empty bottle of bourbon and a half-filled glass. He ignored me long enough to bring the glass to his lips and sip the liquor it contained, his eyes staring vacantly at the floor.

Undaunted, I moved one of the other chairs next to him and sat, leaning toward him. "What happened, Dr. Doherty? And why did you leave the university? Did you perform the experiment?"

He tilted his head and glanced at me. "Too many questions at one time is poor methodology. You should know that fact this late in the game, Daniel."

"Then only one question at a time. Did you perform the experiment?"

"One answer. Yes."

"What happened?"

"I was a child prodigy." He sipped at his glass again. "Did you know that? Did I ever tell you?"

I told him I couldn't remember, and then he regaled me with his personal history. Thomas Doherty had learned to read at three years old, had gotten his first degree at fourteen, his first doctoral degree at nineteen. Early in his academic career he followed several interests, computer science, sociology, biology, physics. He could have chosen any of those fields in which to earn his reputation, but had chosen sociology against the advice of his professors. Why the soft sciences when he displayed such genius for the hard sciences and technology?

In the close, still air of the living room, he didn't wait for me to guess.

"Since I was a child," he said, brandishing his glass like a scepter, "I had one abiding goal. To be able to predict the future of the species with absolute clarity and accuracy. Can you imagine? What do we have on this Earth, seventy, eighty years of life if we're fortunate? No man will ever live long enough to know the zenith of human evolution. It's a logical impossibility. No man lives forever."

But one man *could* know, I thought, and let the rest of the world know, if he found the right mathematical model, if he formulated the right algorithms in a highly advanced computer simulation program that would give him the information necessary to see for himself—

"I spent long years of my life developing my technique of nested algorithms," he said, his eyes recapturing the disarming sharpness he often used as an intellectual weapon against his detractors. "If my programming was sound, and the data sets I used as the basis for my evolutionary model proved accurate, then I could accomplish just that. And I did."

"Then our data sets were accurate?"

"Beautifully accurate, Daniel. I congratulate you and your colleagues on all your hard work in helping me reach the terminus of my lifelong pursuits."

With this pronouncement, he leaned forward and hurled the glass across the room toward the mantle of the fireplace where it shattered noisily into fragments. Then he turned to me and smiled. "Salute!"

I fought to keep my nerve; hearing that my data sets were successfully employed heartened me, if I could only convince Doherty to release his results. Didn't he know my academic future was on the line?

"Why didn't you announce your results, Dr. Doherty? If you've waited most of your life—"

"There lies the paradox, doesn't it?"

"What happened? What did you find?"

"The future." His eyes once again glossed over, as if he'd seen a horribly disheartening vision. "Our future, the future of our species. It was no good. No good at all. And it's going to happen."

"Again, what did you find?"

"You can't unsee something like that, you know? You just can't *unsee* it. What's the point of anything else?"

I didn't know, couldn't possibly know the results of his experiment, but I did know that no scientist should willfully withhold pertinent scientific discoveries from the world. I explained this philosophy to Doherty as he sat staring at me through bloodshot eyes; I implored him, reasoned with him, impelled him to release his findings, and not just in support of my dissertation. The world should know his results. Scientific integrity demanded he release his findings.

Doherty listened patiently to my pleading, perhaps impressed by my eloquence, perhaps not. When my diatribe concluded, he smiled grimly and nodded, evidently realizing something he hadn't before. Then he picked up the bottle of bourbon and drank from it, unconcerned by his base behavior.

"The individual sections of my experiment are all encrypted," he said. "The nested data sets, the primary program, the prime data sets and that damned animation. You'd need the intelligence department of a first world nation to break any one of those encryptions, and even if you broke one you'd be no closer to breaking the others. No, those files are never going to see the light of day."

"But you could have deleted your files instead of leaving them encrypted on the server. You did that for a reason, ambivalence perhaps. Or perhaps you knew you might return to your work—"

He laughed. "You're right. Ambivalence is the devil on my shoulder. I wanted no one else to examine my work, but I also couldn't destroy a lifetime of studies so easily. Could you? I could no more delete those files than kill off my own child, if I had one. But they may as well be deleted. So much for sentimentality."

"So you're just going to turn your back on me and everyone else who gave up a part of their lives to help you," I said, frustrated by his complete lack of caring. "You're going to let us hang in the wind while you drink yourself to death out in the weeds."

He nodded. "I understand why you're angry. Completely. And I'm going to help you understand the reason why I had to shut everything down. Follow me."

Doherty rose unsteadily and walked through the house into a small office. He sat in a chair before an expensive walnut desk while I stood watching him and found a piece of paper and a pen. Patiently writing through his inebriation, he finally concluded his task and handed me the paper. Though I studied his notation carefully, I couldn't interpret it: parentheses full of numbers and lattice-like symbols followed by parentheses of nested numbers and more lattice-like symbols.

"Find Allison Gayheart," he said. "Tell her to open 'File 12' using this key. She'll be able to use it within my mainframe partition. Then you'll both know my rationale for silencing my project."

I wondered if this key might help her puzzle out the encryption on his other files, but he seemed to read my thoughts.

"This key will only work for File 12," he said, grinning. "The other files are bounded by much more rigorous encryption. Believe me, Daniel, you don't want to know the results of the project. The future they depict is real. As real as this."

Doherty pulled open the drawer at his midriff and retrieved a .38 revolver from inside. He placed the weapon on the desk by the notepad he'd used before regarding me. "All my life I searched for the perfect synthesis of organism, environment, and technology. And what did I find?"

I stared at the piece of paper again, then at the gun on his desk. "You shouldn't be alone in this house, Dr. Doherty. Come back to the city with me. We'll find you help."

"Better leave me to my privacy now, Daniel, before I use this gun on *you*."

The next day, toward the afternoon, I managed to track down Allison.

After examining Doherty's note, she agreed that he'd found an ingenious method for nesting the elements of his encryption passwords—one equation must be solved before the missing value for the next could be known. And the latticework symbols baffled her. Without Doherty's initial solution, the key would be useless. When I asked her if this one key could be used to ascertain the basis of the others she laughed and asked me if I knew any genius cryptographers.

When she convinced the lab administrator to let us have access to Dr. Doherty's partition, we settled into the smaller lab room in front of a holographic screen and she brought up File 12. Doherty's sense of the dramatic annoyed me, though my curiosity superseded all other considerations. I still felt guilty for leaving the man alone in the country in a disturbed frame of mind, but admitting my intrusion on his privacy to the authorities just to assuage my conscience over the precarious state of his mental health might have gotten me censured. I was certain he would recover his composure eventually, no matter the unsettling visions conjured by his experiment.

Allison pushed her glasses up against her nose and began methodically entering the key, which involved punching in prefatory numbers which in turn revealed the corresponding latticework symbols which she carefully selected.

After a moment, the screen fluttered noisily, and then a legend appeared on a gray field: FINAL CALCULUS: DR. THOMAS DOHERTY. The legend faded.

And Dr. Thomas Doherty's ashen face manifested.

He'd recorded himself from within his office, his hands together on his desk, his fingers interlaced, a white lab coat, disheveled, hanging from his shoulders—his expression, desperately attempting to retain professional dignity, kept falling to distress, or perhaps despair. He stared into the recorder for a full minute before speaking, first clearing his throat, and then self-consciously straightening in his chair.

"I have completed my review of the experiment's results," he said, his voice washed of its usual assuredness. "And I—" Now he stared vacantly, perhaps trying to find the right words to state his position. "I have come to the conclusion that the experiment has successfully predicted the evolutionary progression of the human species. My calculus functioned perfectly, as I always believed it would. That the experiment succeeded as intended is a moot point, since its results are nothing close to the outcome I envisioned."

Doherty shifted in his chair again, wiping perspiration from his jawline before continuing. "I had always believed that an intelligent species, *any* intelligent species, should exhibit an upward trend of art, culture, and science, and that at the pinnacle of its development, its social relationship with higher philosophical pursuits should be reflected in its achievements. That our use of the sciences would enhance our biology, our philosophical purity. Apparently, this is not the case. It's not even close to being the case.

"Only one letter distinguishes the word evolution from *devolution*, and I let my enthusiasm for humanity's future blind me to the possibility that one would lead to the other. I didn't foresee that all our intelligence, all our scientific and technical skills were only leading to a devolved state of grace as destructive as any animal creating its own oblivion within an exhausted environment. A created human environment is no different, I'm afraid. In fact, it's much, much worse."

Now Doherty's lips began trembling, but he managed to recover his composure.

"We, as a species," he said, "are not destined for utopia. Quite the contrary. A young, intelligent species, still full of hope for the future, shouldn't know that future if it's one of profound disillusionment. Therefore, despite the technical success of my experiment, I have decided that the essential results, if viewed by an academic audience, would result either in complete denial, or in the acceptance of a future so ugly it wouldn't be worth exploring. I can only prevent either outcome by ensuring that the results of my experiment are never examined by another human being."

Now Doherty gazed straight ahead and sighed. "My own disillusionment is death sentence enough."

Then the recording faded to gray.

"That's all," Allison said, sitting back in her chair.

After a moment I asked, "What could have affected him so negatively? What could his results have shown?"

"I wish I knew. Considering the ego of a man like Doherty, they must have been pretty frightening."

I wondered if the future of humanity could be so horrendous—enough to turn Doherty's mind and inspire him to abandon his academic career. And I simply couldn't accept that some projection of events could be so psychologically devastating that merely examining the contents of his files would obliterate a person's hope for the future. After all, his results were only based on a progressive model—

"Allison," I said, "is there any way to extrapolate the key to the other files from the key he gave you for this one? There must be some way of breaking the encryption on the rest."

Before she could respond, another voice answered my question.

"No, there isn't."

We turned to find Doherty standing in the threshold of the lab's doorway, dressed in the same clothes in which I'd found him the previous day, his eyes red, his hair unkempt. The smile on his lips belied the somber mood he'd exhibited in his living room, but his body language clearly still retained his defiance of the world. His sudden intrusion unnerved me, and I remembered the pistol he'd pulled from his desk drawer, hoping he'd left it behind.

"The encryption," he said, moving into the lab on the legs of a man who'd clearly been imbibing, "is based on a series of one million symbols emulating a crystalline structure. Like snowflakes. No two snowflakes are ever alike? Do you remember that little gem from grade school? I personally programmed my own encryption language into the university's mainframe. Well, compound the possible permutations of symbol combinations and the number of possible solutions becomes *astronomical*. You'd sooner be able to count all the atoms in the observable universe than run through all the possible combinations."

Doherty stood next to me, shaking his head. "So unless I provide the keys, no one will *ever* be able to break the encryption on those files."

I glanced uneasily at Allison before addressing him. "Dr. Doherty, I just can't imagine that the results of the experiment would be so disturbing that you would—"

"That's the problem, Daniel," he said, still smiling, "*you* can't imagine. The experiment imagined the future for all of us, and one person seeing that future is one person too many. You wouldn't be able to withstand its effects any better than me. Trust me, I'm doing the world a favor."

"I don't understand," Allison said. "What could be so horrible? Could our future be any more disturbing than the worlds imagined by Dante or Hieronymus Bosch? Why the theatrics?"

"Why indeed?" Doherty said. "What *could* be so horrible, Allison? What possible future could be so bad that a man like me would turn his back on his career and crawl into a bottle? Can you imagine?"

"We're not children," I said, standing to face him. "Listen, I don't care what kind of mental breakdown you're currently experiencing, but you're taking the rest of your research team into the bottle with you. And that's not fair. Nothing could be so problematic that would justify withholding your research and sabotaging the work of your doctoral students. How can you justify any of it?"

Doherty didn't seem offended at all by my words. He only nodded, seeming to consider my question for a long moment before waving Allison out of her chair. She rose and stepped away, probably as bewildered as me, as he clumsily sat in the vacated chair before the console.

"Nothing could be so problematic?" he said, his fingers moving over the keyboard so quickly I couldn't follow his input. "You both believe you're psychologically capable of accepting the results of my experiment. Which is what I'd expect you to say, since you're desperate to save your theses. You'd do anything to try to unlock my files just to promote your academic careers. Well, I can't say I never felt the same way. In fact, my extraordinary ambition led to just this moment. So now I'll have to do you both a favor."

Again his fingers tapped at the keyboard, and I leaned over his shoulder to try to follow his commands which filled the screen with innumerable baffling lines of letters, numbers, and symbols.

Suddenly, a series of file names appeared on the screen before us—files numbered 1 through 12, all highlighted—then, after his fingers moved over the keyboard again, all the file names vanished.

"What did you do?" Allison barked as she leaned toward the console. "Damn it, Doherty!"

Dr. Doherty said, "I erased the files and overwrote all their sectors. A failsafe I personally coded into the mainframe. As far as the world is concerned, my experiment's files never existed."

Stunned, I could only manage a one-word question. "Why?"

He turned, his eyes watery, his face expressing his undisguised pain. "It was so beautifully rendered, Daniel. So beautifully achieved. And so very *ugly*. I couldn't let the rest of the world see the ugliness awaiting us. You have to realize—my entire life lay contained in those files. My work was like a child to me. I didn't want to. But I had to kill it. I *had* to. Every parameter leading toward one overriding social principle—"

"Dr. Doherty," Allison said resignedly, "how ugly could humanity's future possibly be for you to destroy all our work?"

He turned to glance at her, his eyes unfocused. "Dante? Hieronymus Bosch? Do you think primitive artists had the capability to imagine as deeply as a supercomputer, Allison? You just don't understand, you can't, any more than Dante or Bosch could have projected their imaginations into humanity's future. You couldn't, your intellect, *our* intellects just aren't developed enough. In order to answer your question, humanity would have to have developed the intellectual ability to understand a completely unprecedented definition for the concept of—*cannibalism.*"

Then Doherty began crying, softly, and didn't stop even after campus security responded to our call. A medical crew transported him to the hospital. I never spoke to him again.

Since the files no longer existed, and couldn't be retrieved—Doherty's skills as an encryption specialist were nonpareil—my doctoral research had effectively died with them. Allison accepted that afternoon as the unfortunate conclusion of Doherty's as yet undiagnosed mental illness and continued resolutely with her studies. Starting my doctoral research over again seemed my only alternative, under the circumstances, but I couldn't stop thinking about Doherty's experiment, and whether or not he actually succeeded.

And if he had, and the results were as grotesque as he believed, should I abandon my own naïve beliefs in a bright future for our species? Some nights I dream of breaking the encryption on his files to see for myself a future no member of a young, hopeful, intelligent species should see—and I wake up cursing myself for having such faith in the efficacy of the work that the other graduate students and I contributed to the success of Doherty's results.

THE NEWLING

Paul Stansbury

Gertruda caught the newborn as it emerged. Her eyes widened. "A newling female, born in the veil on the full Frost Moon. Wiedźma will be most interested." She removed the caul from the infant's head, carefully setting it aside, then cut the umbilical cord and tied it with a soft woolen thread. "Now to keep you warm, I'll wrap you tightly, so you won't miss the womb."

Juliste held out her arms. "Welcome, Renia," she said, cradling her daughter. "Stefek, she has your curly hair, though I have no idea why it is red."

"Go now, veštica," Stefek growled at Gertruda, throwing some coins on the table, "and leave us in peace."

Gertruda stiffened. "Watch your tongue. I am not a witch. Out of the kindness of my heart, did I come." She had arrived at sunset the evening before, scratching at the door like a hungry animal, and spent the night tending to Juliste.

"You are well paid," grumbled Stefek. "And a liar. Everyone knows you are Wiedźma's acolyte first and a midwife second."

"You were the one who called for me."

Stefek hung his head. "I wish I hadn't."

"What you wish is of no consequence to me. I would have come anyway. No birth escapes my scrutiny and consequently that of Wiedźma. Did you ever consider that what I do is in the interest of the village? Without me, she would visit every birth and that would be disastrous. She can be a most unwelcome guest."

"Damn you to hell, veštica. You care not a whit about this village, only yourself and your ghastly mistress."

No, no, no. She is dangerous. "Stefek, please don't aggravate her," begged Juliste.

Gertruda cocked her head, glaring at Stefek. "Would you have delivered it with those rough, clumsy, woodcutter's hands? Delivering a newling is not like digging turnips or splitting logs. Would that I could leave and put you behind me, woodcutter. But there is yet more to do. Your wife has not given up the afterbirth. After it comes, I will leave."

I've got to get Stefek out of here before he does something foolish. "It's cold in here, dear husband. Please get some wood for the fire, so Renia will be warm."

Stefek jumped to his feet, clenching his fists. He drew in a deep breath before pulling on his gloves and coat. Cold, musty air swirled around the tiny dwelling as he squeezed out the door. Juliste pulled a rough woolen blanket over Renia.

"A wise decision," sniggered Gertruda.

Juliste and she sat in silence until Stefek re-entered, arms laden with wet, dripping firewood. He dropped the split logs in a jumbled heap on the dirt floor, then closed the door. Placing a couple of splits on the fire, he stacked the rest on the side. The damp wood hissed and popped in the flames. Gray smoke floated up through an opening in the thatched roof.

In the meantime, as Juliste breastfed Renia, Gertruda began to harvest the afterbirth.

Stefek watched her gather the spent flesh. "What do you intend to do with that?" he asked.

"I will take it to Wiedźma."

"For what foul purpose?'

"Because she wants to examine it."

"You and the mistress you serve are abominations."

"Watch your words," Gertruda warned, staring into Stefek's eyes, "Wiedźma does not tolerate such talk. Know this, woodcutter, she cares nothing about you and your wretched wife, only the newling. Now, I must take this to her," she said, holding up the afterbirth, "for her decision."

"And what will that be?" asked Juliste.

"It is not up to me."

Stefek rubbed his forehead. "Can't you show some discretion? Some mercy? Does Wiedźma even have to know? Why not say the baby was stillborn? I can pay. I have more money."

Gertruda paused, raising a bloody hand. She pulled back the hood from her head, revealing ragged scars peeking through her oily hair, running down the side of her head. "This was my reward for discretion." She yanked the hood back up. "Keep your money."

"But Renia is our firstborn," Juliste pleaded.

"All the more reason," taunted Gertruda. "Make sure to feed it well."

"No, you can't have her," Stefek shouted, pounding the table with his fist.

"Enough talk," Gertruda said, standing up. "Your whining has no sway with me." She stuffed the afterbirth in the pouch hanging from her shoulder, then looked out the window. The light of the full moon had faded into a gray dawn. "Wiedźma is waiting. If she wishes to take the newling, we will return on the full Wolf Moon." Gertruda paused, pointing to the baby Juliste clutched to her breast. "And make sure it stays safe, and don't try to run away. You can't hide." She patted the pouch. "We have the newling's scent and Wiedźma will find the newling no matter how far you run."

Stefek stood up and took a step toward Gertruda. Pulling a knife from his belt, he growled, "And what if you suddenly disappear?"

"No," cried Juliste.

Gertruda laughed. "Wiedźma can be exquisitely cruel if she doesn't get what she desires. She will take her revenge not only on you, but everyone in this village."

"Let her go, Stefek," pleaded Juliste. "We can't stain Renia's birth with this woman's blood."

"And no priests," hissed Gertruda, wagging a crooked finger. She slid past Stefek and out the door, muttering, "No, no. She doesn't like priests and their holy water."

Stefek watched Gertruda shuffle off, her muddy footprints fading under the melting sleet. When he was sure she would not turn back, he closed the door and turned to Juliste. "What are we to do? I would rather that Renia had never been born than to have to face this."

"It has been born," whispered Gertruda, head bowed. She knelt in the icy muck and decaying vegetation of the bog, offering a bloody clump of flesh to the gaunt, one-eyed giantess.

Sniffing the air, Wiedźma focused her bloodshot eye on the midwife. "First born, female?"

"Yes."

"Born on the full Frost Moon?"

"Yes, and born with a veil."

"Ahh," rasped Wiedźma. She climbed down from her perch atop a moss-covered rock, gray, crepey skin dragging over deformed bones. Reaching out with a gnarled hand, she raked a jagged fingernail across the afterbirth, allowing a trickle of sticky blood to coat her quivering fingers. Her long, snake tongue slithered out and licked them clean. "And the veil?"

Gertruda pulled the caul from her pouch, holding it out. "Perfect," hissed Wiedźma. "Return to your village. Tell the woman when the Wolf Moon is full, I will come to fetch the newling. And tell her not to spare her teats. I want the newling fattened up when I take it."

A week crawled by. The fall winds howled, and slate clouds filled the sky, weeping cold rain and sleet. Clouds also filled the souls of Juliste and Stefek.

"Winter will be here soon, and we will be snowed in. There is not enough wood to make it through." said Stefek. "Everyone in the village has been asking when I will bring more." He stared at the fire's glowing red coals. "I know I must, but the thought of leaving you and Renia alone is unbearable."

"We will be fine. Everyone depends on you." Juliste put her arms around Stefek, burying her head in his chest. "Renia and I depend on you. Can you cut enough before the Wolf Moon is full?"

Stefek stroked her long black hair. "I can make three trips to the south wood between now and then. That will last a long time. It will have to."

"Then you must go immediately."

Stefek fell silent. "I am ashamed. I am not a worthy husband. To leave you and Renia now is cowardly."

Juliste, touched his cheek. "But you cannot abandon your responsibilities to the village. There are other mothers and children here who will suffer if they do not have wood to burn when the ice comes."

"I should have found a way to prevent this, but I am weak and afraid. I fear our situation is hopeless. Wiedźma will come for Renia, I am sure."

"Gertruda said the beast would, but you must remain strong if not for yourself or me, then for Renia."

"Juliste, you are our strength," he said.

"You must promise not to give up hope. The time may come when you will have to be strong for all of us."

"Yes, my love."

At dawn the following morning, Stefek set off for the south wood with two ox-drawn sledges. Juliste fought back tears as she watched him disappear into the gray mist. She caressed Renia's cheek. "He will be back soon, little one." *What am I to do?*

Juliste was about to close the door when she heard someone call out. "I see Stefek has gone off to cut wood." She looked down the path to see an old woman hobbling toward her.

"Yes. Is that you, Ruta?"

"Yes."

"He has gone to the south wood."

"Good," Ruta panted, "I have come to see the baby." She paused. "And, I have something I wish to speak with you about."

Juliste waited until Ruta reached the door. "Will you come in and warm yourself by the fire?"

"Thank you. I can miss no opportunity to warm these old bones."

Juliste pulled a stool close to the fire for the old woman. "There is some barszcz left from breakfast. Would you like some? It will warm you most comfortably."

"Please. You are so kind. But first, I must see..."

"Renia," said Juliste, handing her to Ruta.

"Ahh, the pure one," she whispered, caressing Renia's cheek. "So beautiful, how old is she?"

"She was born eight days ago."

"That would be on the full Frost Moon, wouldn't it?"

Juliste frowned, recalling the encounter with Gertruda. "Yes."

"Is it safe to assume that Gertruda attended?"

Juliste stiffened. "Yes. Shall I put Renia in the cradle and get your soup?"

"Yes, dear," Ruda said, handing Renia back to Juliste.

Juliste laid Renia in the cradle, then ladled some sour hogweed soup into a bowl and handed it to Ruta. "I can also offer you some flatbread and salt."

"Thank you for your generous offer, but this will be all." Ruta took a sip and smiled. "Good soup. May this home be blessed."

"You are welcome at our fire. You said you wanted to speak with me."

"Did Gertruda tell you Wiedźma will come for Renia?"

None of your business. Juliste lowered her head. "Yes."

Ruta put her hand on Julista's arm. "I know what you and Stefek face." Juliste's arm tightened under her hand. "I do not come to pry into your affairs, but please hear me out." Juliste nodded. Ruta continued, "Many years ago, my daughter faced the same plight as you face now. Try as they might, she and her husband could find no way to escape the evil designs of Wiedźma. In the end, they gave up."

Juliste fought back tears. "What happened?"

"As to the fate of the child, I do not know. As for my daughter and her husband, they came to sad endings. After a few months, her husband drifted off."

"And your daughter?"

Ruta bowed her head, then whispered, "A short time later, she hung herself."

"I am sorry."

Ruta brushed the comment away with a swipe of her hand. "It is best not to dwell in the past. Since then, I have searched for a way to rid the world of Wiedźma in the hope that what happened to my daughter will not happen to anyone else. Had I known then what I know now, her story might have ended differently."

"What do you mean?"

"A whisperer lives high in the forbidden hills. She can cast spells and charms, and free people from evil possessions. I have spoken with her and I believe if anyone can find a way to defeat Wiedźma, it is she."

What craziness is this? Juliste frowned, looking at Renia, sleeping in her cradle. "I don't know."

"Have you found a way to stop Wiedźma?"

"No."

"Do you want to save Renia?" Juliste nodded, then began to sob. "Then, you must go."

"What will she do?"

"That, she would not share with me." Ruta placed a hand on Juliste's shoulder. "That is all the szeptucha said, dear. Her name is Celina. You will find a path behind the blacksmith's forge. It will lead you into the forbidden hills. Stay on the path and she will find you. " Ruta stood up. "I will leave you now. You have a decision to make."

Juliste had made her decision—two in fact.

Stefek had sharpened his axes the night before, and by the light of his lantern, hitched the oxen to the sledges. Juliste packed some flatbread and smoked cheese in his haversack.

She hugged him tightly. "Will you be back before the new moon?"

"Don't worry, dear," he said, kissing her face. He hefted an ax. "I have had a lot of time while woodcutting to think about things. When I return, I will have a use for this other than chopping wood."

"What do you mean?"

"I mean to confront this Wiedźma, and kill her."

"No, Stefek. It's too dangerous."

"Danger aside, it is the only thing that will end this nightmare. I have faced danger before. When I was fourteen, I killed a brown bear with an ax. Surely this Wiedźma is no stronger than a bear. I will kill her and Gertruda too, and the village will be rid of them for good. Do not try to dissuade me. I have made up my mind." He scooped Juliste up with one arm and twirled her around. "See how strong your husband is. I pity Wiedźma."

Juliste let out a gleeful shriek, then buried her face against his neck, fighting back her tears. "Be safe Stefck. Don't do anything foolish, a way to defeat Wiedźma may yet be found."

He kissed her. "As I said, I have already found it. Come, wife. Let us have a proper goodbye before I leave."

As dawn's first light broke, Stefek set out for his third and final trip to gather wood before the full Wolf Moon rose. Juliste waited for an hour to make sure he was well beyond the village before she set out to find Celina. She had decided not to tell Stefek she was going.

"We will not burden your father with this," Juliste said to Renia. "He has enough to think about. Besides, I am only going to listen to what this Celina has to say. If I don't like it, I shall find some other way to defeat Wiedźma." She bundled Renia within her cloak.

Finding the path behind the blacksmith's forge, she began her journey into the forbidden hills. The path rose steadily up steep, tree-covered slopes. Slick, damp leaves threatened to send her feet sliding out from under her, and she found the going arduous. Stopping to suck in a breath, she looked up through the bare branches. Black cracks in a stone sky.

Well into the day, the path ran out, leaving Juliste exhausted and alone among the imposing trees. Within her cloak, Renia squirmed. "Are you hungry, little one?" Juliste asked, sitting down and leaning back on a thick oak. She pulled her blouse up and guided Renia to her breast. While her baby suckled, Juliste softly sang a lullaby.

Sleep my baby, Renia,
Peacefully sleep.
Your mother will gently kiss you.

Don't be afraid of dragons,
Your mother will protect you.

Soon, Juliste fell into a fitful sleep, her mind swirling with dark dreams.

Juliste was awakened by a tap on her shoulder. She opened her eyes to find a short woman dressed in a green cloak standing before her. Curly auburn hair flowed over her shoulders. She held a staff in one hand and a lantern in the other.

"You must be Juliste. Ruta said you might come in search of me."

Juliste placed a hand on the hilt of her knife while she gazed into the woman's bright green eyes. "Are you Celina?"

"I am the one you seek. You and your child have no need to fear me."

Juliste relaxed. "Then you know why I have come."

"Yes. But this is no place to talk. Soon it will be dark and little moonlight will reach us under the trees. Follow me." Celina set off into the dusky woods. Soon, all Juliste could see was Celene's black silhouette moving forward in the amber glow of the lantern. They walked on for some time until Celina stopped. Juliste peeked around her and saw a small round hut in the dim lantern light. Juliste drew back.

"What, you think I'm the Baba Jaga," laughed Celina. She pushed open the door. "You may come in and sit by my hearth, or stay out here in the cold."

Juliste hesitated before finally entering. Celina tossed off her cloak, then stirred up the coals in the fireplace. She tossed on some wood and soon a bright blaze popped up.

"Have some nettle tea and a seed cake? You must be hungry after your journey."

"Yes," said Julista, pulling off her cloak. She loosened the blanket she had wrapped around Renia.

"Will you give her to me?" asked Celina.

Juliste cocked her head and stared at the woman.

"You see, It has been a very long time since I held an infant," said Celina. Juliste hesitated, then placed Renia in her outstretched hands. Celina stroked Renia's cheek. "You will have green eyes like mine. Rest easy. We shall stop those who would come like the wild wolves to take you away."

Juliste buried her face in her hands and sobbed.

"Wiedźma and her acolyte can be stopped, and this child saved," said Celina. "That is if you have the will to do it."

"I will do anything to save Renia."

"So be it. Remember though, anything sometimes takes much courage and sacrifice. Now, get some sleep. Tomorrow we have much to do."

Wiedźma focused her rheumy eye on the waxing gibbous moon and cackled. She crept down from her rock. Leaning over, nose almost touching the ground, she searched for the scent. "Ah, there you are," she sighed, a smile cracking her gray withered face. Knotted, twisted fingers raked away the vegetation and icy muck, revealing the decaying afterbirth Gertruda had buried.

Wiedźma inhaled its putrid odor. "Soon, very soon, you will be mine. In the morning, Gertruda will come, and we will prepare for my journey to find you," she growled.

Celina shook Juliste's shoulder, waking her from a troubled sleep. "Come child, we have much to do in the few days remaining before the full Wolf Moon rises." Juliste found Renia snuggled to her breast. She sat up, looking at Celina, wondering if it had all been a dream. "Feed your child, she is hungry," said Celina, "and eat something yourself." She handed Juliste a seed cake. "You have work to do before this day is done."

"And what might that be?" Juliste asked. She pulled up her blouse for Renia to feed. The tingly, warm sensation of her letdown put Juliste at ease.

"You remember our conversation?"

Juliste felt a pang of anxiety. "Yes."

"And you are still willing to do this?"

Juliste's chest tightened. *Run. Take Renia and run now—from Celina—from Gertruda—from Wiedźma—from the dreadful fate that awaits. Run until Renia, Stefek and I are far from this grim valley, where we never will be found.* The thought of Wiedźma taking Renia paralyzed her body. Horrific images roiled inside her brain. Lungs burning, she gasped for breath. Finally realizing flight was impossible, she whispered, "Yes."

Celina poured some barley tea in a cup and handed it to Juliste. "Finish this and eat your cheese. You will need your strength for you have an errand to undertake.

"What is that?"

"Deep in the forest, there is a spring. The water flowing from it is pure. You must bring some back. Along the way, you will find a krzywa dąb—"

"A crooked oak?"

"Yes, bring an acorn from this tree. It must be one still hanging from a branch, not one that has touched the ground. Do you understand? It cannot have touched the ground."

"I understand. What is all this for?"

"I will explain everything when you get back. Eat up now, there is much to be done."

After Juliste finished her meager breakfast, Celina led her outside. She handed her a large gourd. "Fill this with the spring water. Do not drink from it. The water must be pure."

"Yes. Where do I find the oak and the spring?"

"This way," Celina said. Juliste followed her around the hut to a path that trailed off into the forest. "This will lead you to the spring. Halfway there, you will find the crooked oak. Remember to pick an acorn from its branch, not one from the ground. Go on till you find the spring. Fill your gourd, but do not drink from it. The water must be pure. Come straight back."

While Juliste was away, Celina returned to her hut and took some ashes from the hearth and placed them in a stone mortar.

Next, she gathered an array of pokes and pouches filled with herbs and other concoctions. Going outside, she put them in a semicircle on the ground. Next, she cut some nettles, careful to preserve the stalks.

The afternoon was waning when Juliste returned. She found Celina sitting on the ground outside her hut, playing a flute. "Where is Renia?"

"She is asleep. You found the crooked oak and the spring?" Celina asked.

"Yes."

"You did not drink from the gourd nor allow the acorn to touch the ground?"

"Yes. Now what is this all about?"

"An odmieniec."

Juliste wrinkled her brow. "A changeling? For what purpose?"

"To fool Wiedźma, of course."

Juliste rubbed her forehead, while tears welled up in her eyes. "I am the fool. I have suffered your follies only to be told the solution is to fool Wiedźma with a changeling. I'm taking Renia away from here."

Celina's eyes blazed. "Wait. You will be the fool if you give up when we are so close. You cannot escape Wiedźma, nor can you defeat her on your own. In your heart, you know this is the truth. A cruel death awaits all of you if you leave now."

"But, how can Wiedźma be defeated with a changeling?"

"She is a greedy, evil creature who believes no one can defeat her. This is her weakness. She will not suspect the surprise you will have in store for her."

"Why hasn't anyone done this before now?"

Celina paused. "Perhaps the opportunity never presented itself. Perhaps no one has had the faith and strength to stay the course."

"Why does it fall to me and my family?"

"Fate neither favors nor curses any person. Sometimes, bad things happen to good folk while bad folk live long, comfortable, privileged lives. We have no say in what fate chooses for us, but we can choose our path through it. Go see Renia while you think about this."

Juliste handed Celina the gourd and acorn before she entered the hut. Inside, Renia was sleeping peacefully in a large dough bowl resting on the floor near the hearth. Juliste knelt beside her, holding her cold hands out to catch the warmth of the fire.

Renia stirred. Juliste picked her up and held her tight. Gently pulling back her cradle blanket, she kissed Renia on the forehead. "Don't worry little one," she whispered. "You will not be with Celina too long."

Before she could say anything else, Celina called. "Come child, we have work to do." Juliste laid Renia down and stepped outside. Celina was waiting with a hoe. Holding it out, she pointed to a patch of grass near the edge of the forest. "Dig a short trench."

"A short trench?" asked Juliste.

"Make it big enough to bury the changeling."

"You mean you're going to bury it? What good will that do?"

Celina shook her head. "Do not run ahead of yourself. You will understand in due time. For now, you dig while I make the other preparations." Juliste took the hoe and began tearing furiously at the earth. In her mind, she was chopping Gertruda and Wiedźma into small pieces. She wanted to bury them and free her family from this wicked curse. If only it were that easy. While Juliste worked, Celina played a strange and wandering melody on her flute. It did nothing to calm Juliste's ragged nerves. She continued digging until her muscles ached.

Celina pulled the flute from her lips. "That will do," she said.

Juliste set the hoe aside, then sat on the ground. "What now?"

"Go be with Renia. She will be hungry. When you are finished, we make the changeling." Celina brought the flute to her lips and began to play. Juliste went inside and picked Renia up. She sat down in Celina's rocking chair. As Renia suckled, Juliste rocked while singing a lullaby.

Lullay, lullay, my tiny child,
Too soon you'll know the world so wild,
Yes, all too soon, you will be gone.
And I'll bide elsewhere, alone, alone.
But yet awhile, with you, I'll stay.
Lullay my sweet one, my child, lullay.

Juliste didn't bother to wipe away her tears before she drifted to sleep.

The tears on her cheeks had long since dried by the time Celina appeared in the doorway to awaken her. "Come child, we have little time left this day to do what must be done. After we finish, you will have the night to spend with Renia. Put some wood on the fire to keep her warm." Juliste laid Renia down, careful not to wake her, then put two small logs on the coals. She stepped out into the dusk.

Celina was sitting in the center of the semicircle she had created. Firelight flickered on the mortar she held in her lap. "We'll start with those," she said, pointing to a red pouch. "Bring it here." Juliste retrieved the pouch and held it open. Celina grabbed a small handful of castor beans, which she dropped into the stone bowl. "Now the wild privet," she said, pointing to a blue poke. Juliste picked it up, noticing its sweet, honey-like scent. "Tempting, but most deadly," Celina said, tossing in several berry-laden sprigs.

After something from each pouch and poke had been added. Celina handed the bowl and a stone grinding club to Juliste. "Grind these into a coarse mixture." Juliste sat down, and began to pound and grind the contents. Celina picked up her flute and played.

After some time, Celina said, "That will do. Bring that and come with me." She walked over to the trench Juliste had dug earlier and knelt. Scooping up some soil, she added it to the stone bowl Juliste held, saying, "Mix it in while I lay out the nettles." Juliste mixed while Celina placed the acorn in the middle of the trench, then arranged the nettles around it, creating a stick figure. "Give me the bowl," Celina said. She poured some water from the gourd to form a thick paste which she mounded on the nettles to form a small, crude mud figure. She looked up at Juliste. "Fetch Renia."

Juliste gasped. "Why?"

"We need her to complete the changeling. No harm will come to her, I promise." Juliste hesitated, then walked to the hut. Celina waited until she returned with Renia held close to her bosom. "Let me see her hand," said Celina. Juliste pulled back the cradle blanket, freeing Renia's tiny arm. "Hold her over the changeling." Juliste edged up to the trench. Before she could react, Celina grabbed Renia's hand and pricked it with a bone needle. Renia wailed as a drop of blood fell on the mud figure.

Juliste backed away crying out, "What have you done?"

"It was a small prick, but a necessary one. Wiedźma will not be fooled unless the changeling carries Renia's blood scent," she paused, staring intently at Juliste, "and yours." Juliste glared at the woman. "You have come this far, do not give up now, we are so close." Renia had stopped crying and only the sounds of the woodland creatures could be heard. Juliste glared at Celina, then stepped forward, holding her hand out. Celina grabbed it and drew a knife across her palm. Blood welled up from the wound, spilling onto the changeling. "There," said Celina, reaching into her pocket and pulling out a small poultice. "This will staunch the bleeding. Take Renia back inside while I finish things here."

After Juliste left, Celina raked the remaining soil back into the trench, covering the changeling. She poured the water remaining in the gourd over the soil, then joined Juliste.

Wiedźma sat atop her rock. She sniffed the air, recognizing the stale, sour odor of Gertruda. She would arrive soon.

Gertruda wrapped a threadbare shawl around her hood to keep the bitter wind's sting off her face. The full Wolf Moon was near, and she had ventured into the bog to accompany her mistress to the village. It meant spending several nights in the cold, whipping wind.

The sun was low in the sky when Gertruda genuflected before Wiedźma. Her knee sunk into freezing muck. She stayed there; head bowed until her mistress spoke.

"Is the newling still alive?"

"She was there when I left two days ago, and I have no reason to suspect anything has changed," Gertruda said, standing up.

"Ahh."

"Shall we leave at daybreak?"

"Yes. I am hungry. It has been a long time since I have feasted," grunted Wiedźma. "A newling's flesh is sweet." She licked her lips, then sniffed the air. "It will snow tonight."

Celina played a soft melody on her flute. She set it aside, stirred the coals and laid on two small logs. Soon a cheery blaze popped up and she placed the teakettle at its edge. As the barley tea brewed, she set out a jar of honey and cut two slices of dark bread. She gently nudged Juliste. "Wake up, child. Time for you to return home."

Juliste opened her eyes, rolled over and saw her daughter watching the flames dance in the fireplace. Celina placed a slice of dark bread on a plate and drizzled some honey over it. "Here, eat this. You will need your strength. After you finish, we will harvest the changeling. Then you must be on your way if you wish to return to your village before the full Wolf Moon."

After Juliste finished, Celina led her outside. A light snow had fallen. The early morning sun shining through the trees cast amber streaks on the snow. Already melting, it revealed the hump of dirt where they had buried the changeling. A bright green shoot with a large pod rose from its center. "Ahh, it is ready," said Celina.

"What is ready?"

"The changeling." Celina walked over to the pod and cut it from the stem, which withered and fell to the ground. "Inside, hurry." She trotted off to the hut. Juliste followed.

Inside, Celina laid the pod on her table. She nicked the top with her knife and peeled back the husk, revealing the changeling. Juliste gasped. It looked like Renia but pale, still and lifeless. Celina removed the remaining husk. She lifted its chin with one hand and pinched its nose with the other. Taking a breath, she covered its open mouth with hers, and gently blew. The changeling opened its colorless eyes.

Juliste turned her head away. The sight of the changeling made her mind reel. *This is surely the devil's work.*

"I know what you're thinking," said Celina. "This indeed is a dire thing we do, but necessary under the circumstances. You will take the changeling with you and pretend it is Renia until you give it up to Wiedźma. Then, your work will be completed, and its work will begin. Now you must wrap it in Renia's blanket to carry her scent."

"I can't."

Handing the changeling to Juliste, Celina said, "Hold this." Then, she removed Renia's cradle blanket and handed it to Juliste. "It must have Renia's scent if it is to fool Wiedźma. Wrap the changeling while I find a blanket for Renia. Then you must start your trip home if you are to arrive before Wiedźma comes." After they finished, Celina held out Renia to Juliste. "Say your goodbye, but be quick. You have a long walk home."

"Goodbye?"

"Surely, you realize you can't return to the village with two infants. Renia must stay. Take her with you and Wiedźma will pick up her scent. Don't worry, I will take care of her."

Juliste laid the changeling on the table and took Renia. She turned away from Celina. "Only for a short while, my little one," she whispered. "When Wiedźma is defeated, your father will come for you." She kissed Renia's forehead, then turned to face Celina. "I am ready."

"I know this is hard, but it is the only way," Celina said. "Now, give her to me." Juliste handed Renia over and picked up the changeling. "Don't worry, child." Celina opened the door and pointed east. "Walk toward the sun and in due time, you will find your path."

Juliste had to wait two days for Stefek to return. The next day would bring the full Wolf Moon. On that day, after sunset, Gertruda would come to fetch Wiedźma's prize.

After Stefek had delivered the wood, fed and bedded down his oxen, he returned to his wife and child. Juliste greeted him at the door. He picked her up in his strong arms and kissed her on the lips. "How I have missed you and Renia these past days. Where is she?"

"Sleeping," she said. "Don't wake her. Let me fix you supper."

"I'll have a look at my daughter first," he said, lowering Juliste. He walked over to the cradle and pulled the blanket away from the changeling's face. Juliste held her breath. "She looks pale," he said. "Is anything wrong?"

Juliste knelt beside the cradle, buried her face in her hands and began to cry. "I have something to tell you."

"Why would you do such a foolish thing without telling me?" Stefek raged. "You engage in the devil's work and leave our daughter with a witch and bring that abomination into our home?"

"I believed it to be the only way to save Renia and defeat Wiedźma. We can't defeat her by ourselves. That is for sure. As strong as you are, you would be no match for her. That is why I did what I did. Tomorrow, you will go to fetch Renia. As I returned from Celina's, I marked my way—broken branches, notches in the tree trunks, so you should have no trouble finding her hut. You will bring Renia back here and wait for me. While you are doing that, I will wait for Gertruda. When she takes the changeling to Wiedźma, I will follow. If Celina is right and the changeling kills Wiedźma, then I will return with good news. If not, I will return to warn the village, then we will flee as far as we can. If she finds us, then you can test your ax."

Stefek rubbed his forehead. "I don't like it."

"What other choice do we have?"

Stefek had been gone for hours and the sun was setting when Gertruda came to the door.

"I have come for the newling," she hissed.

"Wait here," said Juliste. "I would rather you didn't enter."

"As you wish, but be quick, Wiedźma does not like to be kept waiting."

Juliste picked up the changeling. She pulled away the cradle cover and kissed it on the forehead. Its skin was cool. She held it tight against her bosom, feigning a mother's love. *I'll be glad to be rid of you.* She turned her head away as she held it out to Gertruda.

"I thought you'd have more pluck about you," she cackled as she took the changeling. "No matter, it makes my task easier."

"Leave now, veštica. May you savor your reward from your beastly mistress."

Gertruda pursed her lips, stared at Juliste, then shook her head. "As you wish," she sneered. She turned and scuffed away.

Juliste waited to see if she would turn around. Satisfied she wouldn't, Juliste donned her cloak and set off to follow her to Wiedźma. The Wolf Moon's light replaced the waning sunlight, making it easy for Juliste to follow Gertruda. She walked steadily north through the forest. Juliste maintained a safe distance. The Wolf Moon reached its zenith as Gertruda stepped into a clearing. In its center, Wiedźma waited. Juliste cringed at the sight of the repulsive, misshapen creature. She hid behind a tree and watched.

Gertruda dropped to one knee. She removed the blanket from the changeling, then held it high above her head. "The Newling."

Wiedźma snatched it from her hands. She held it close to her face, inhaling. "Ahh. I've waited so long for the flesh of a newling." She opened her maw, filled with multiple rows of yellow, jagged teeth, and shoved the changeling in, headfirst. The sound of grinding, tearing flesh filled Juliste's ears. She turned her head away from the gruesome sight and fainted.

Wiedźma swallowed the changeling's flesh with several large gulps. She was licking her fingers when she began to gag in pain. Grabbing Gertruda, she gurgled, "What have you done to me?"

"Nothing, mistress," pleaded Gertruda. "The newling's mother must have done something."

"It burns, it burns," shrieked Wiedźma, clutching at her chest. She swung Gertruda about wildly.

"Please, mistress, put me down. I did nothing wrong," Gertruda pleaded.

"You have poisoned me, traitor," Wiedźma howled. She grabbed Gertruda with both hands, ripping her acolyte in half. Grasping her throat with both hands, she convulsed uncontrollably then toppled to the ground. She moaned, writhing in pain until her body fell still.

Juliste regained consciousness. It was quiet, and the moon was no longer overhead, but touching the treetops. Juliste stood up and looked at the clearing. There, the bodies laid, motionless black heaps. *Was Celina right? Are they really dead?* She picked up a long stick and ventured forward, looking for any sign of movement. None. She approached Gertruda's top half and jabbed it. No response. She moved to Wiedźma. Her snake tongue lay out on the ground. Juliste knew she was dead, but drove the stick deep into her eye until it struck the back of her skull. She turned and started for home.

Juliste had run all night to be there when Stefek returned with Renia.

He returned late in the afternoon. He came through the door and fell to the floor. Juliste knelt down beside Stefek. Tears rolled down her cheeks. "Where is Renia?"

Stefek stared into the embers of the fire. "Followed the path till it ran out. From there, I followed the signs you left till I came to a clearing. It was like you described, but there was no hut, only a bare patch. I searched all around."

"And?"

Stefek pulled Juliste close. "She is gone."

THE SEVEN STAGES OF GRIEF

Diana Olney

A(1. Shock)
Between tongues of flame,
she traces his bones,
an artless dalliance
dipped in gold;
the map of marrow
constellating irradiant
through forked vein and coiled viscera—
a path laid in a nest of serpents.

(2. Denial)
The embers eat well,
while she starves
—a hunger strike in twisted nerves.

Pincushion fingertips
like electric shivers, sweeping
the striations of sunken plateaus,
serrated ridges, frozen
peaks and sepulchered cavities.

(3. Indignation)
There was warmth there, once,
beauty, too,
stark as a cigarette burn,
soft as rose petals,
a wild anachronism
among saw-toothed thorns.
but when a restless soul
begins to cannibalize
pretty things
are the first to go.

(4. The Bargain)
Tonight's spread
   is on the fire:
      an eye
   for an eye.

(5. Melancholy)
Memories in red,
fodder for the blaze,
sparks scintillated with
obscene liaisons.
The anathema
of clawed sheets and jagged
nails emblazoning
fevered vice and secret
scars—
a curse carried
subcutaneous

beneath stilted silence.

(6. Reconstruction)
The conflagration whispers,
tongues lapping susurrant,
while ribs crack in sharp succession.
His echo: rabid, dissonant
—a staccato requiem
in the key of madness.

(7. Acceptance)
At the crescendo,
the heart awaits her final oblation:
a tear cut like glass,
fractal and vitreous,
salting the open wound
of this man,
this cage,
this shadow,
she once called home.
At her side, the flames leap,
hungry for bone.

TO THINE OWN SELF

Kelly S. Hossaini

If you walked into a room and Mortmain Wendell Blevins was standing in it, it would take you a while to notice him. If he was alone in the room, it might be minutes before you became aware that you weren't alone. If the room had other people in it, you might never notice him. His invisibility often startled people in the office lunchroom. One would walk in, assume the room was empty, and then sit down to eat lunch at a table, only to be startled at some point by a sneeze or a cough. How long had he been there? There was nothing particularly unnerving about Morty, as he was called, that you could put your finger on. He just left a general impression of distaste, like a bagel that had been ruined with raisins. He didn't make people recoil with horror, but people instinctively avoided him.

Morty was born to fairly well-to-do parents in a midsize city in a backwater state. He was an only child. His parents both worked for the local school district, one as an unremarkable teacher and the other as an unremarkable administrator. They were both enamored with lawyers and the law, probably because they had never really met any lawyers and never had to expose themselves directly to the law. Morty's parents chose Mortmain as his first name because it sounded sophisticated and legalistic, which it was. Unfortunately, it was French for "dead hand," which wasn't very appetizing. His parents chose Wendell after Oliver Wendell Holmes, who they knew was a famous judge. Blevins, of course, couldn't be helped.

For whatever reason, prior to attending first grade Morty was called "Dell" instead of some derivation of his first name. This changed, however, on Morty's first day of first grade. The teacher was taking roll and calling out the children's names as they appeared in the official school records. The teacher called on Roberts, who became Bobbies, and Jennifers, who became Jennies, and even a Wilfred who became Freddy. Then she called on Mortmain Blevins and after a short silence the class burst into laughter, heads on a swivel, looking at who might be the owner of such a name. Morty blushed deeply and raised his hand as unobtrusively as he could. Then he softly said, "It's Dell." But the other children wouldn't hear of it. They called him Morty and it stuck. Whether this bothered Morty or not, no one could tell. If it did, he betrayed no signs of it.

Morty had in inauspicious school career. He didn't actually wet his pants in the second grade, but everyone believed that he did, so the story stuck to him. As did the story that he puked up a pink liquidy vomit during a field trip to the zoo in the third grade. It was actually one of the Bobbies who had done that, but the kids remembered it as him, so that stuck, too. In high school he disappeared into the audio-visual club (or the A/V Club as it was known) and studied the finer points of operating film projectors, which were already becoming obsolete even as he learned about them.

Morty knew that his parents' big dream for him was that he become a lawyer. He knew that his first and middle names were only the tip of the expectation iceberg. As a family they would watch shows on television that featured lawyers and his parents bought him biographies of famous lawyers and judges. Morty read some of these books and dutifully watched the shows with his parents, but he never felt any real drive to actually become a lawyer. In fact, the best effort he could muster was to take paralegal courses at the local community college whereupon he was hired by a midsize law firm in his midsize city in his backwater state to do litigation support. The work rather suited him actually, because it involved a never-ending flow of documents to be cataloged and superficially reviewed in anticipation of further review by junior associates. The work could be done in relative solitude and he was tireless at it.

Life at the firm was generally full of routine and predictability. This is why Morty liked it so much. Although he worked in the litigation department, his particular duties insulated him from much of the chaotic uncertainty normally associated with a litigation practice. Morty's highly prized routine and predictability changed, however, when the firm hired a new paralegal, Tympany Morgan. Normally, Morty didn't take notice of new hires or even old hires for that matter. He stuck to his business and left other people alone, as they did him. But Tympany Morgan would prove to be different.

Some would characterize Tympany as a 1980s Goth holdover. She had colored her hair jet black and her face was coated with a foundation three shades too light. Black kohl rimmed her eyes. She was very thin and very tall. The first time that Morty noticed her as she passed his office door, all he saw were bare legs extending from a short, black skirt. Shortly thereafter, the legs passed by his office again, doubled back, and then entered. Morty stared uneasily at this woman who stood in his doorway and then swept in, uninvited. He thought she looked kind of like a witch.

"Tympany Morgan," said the witch, extending her skinny arm across his desk. Morty stood up abruptly, still staring at her. He cautiously took the hand and shook it as if it were disembodied.

"Morty . . . Blevins." Cough, throat clearing. Tympany looked around.

"It's dark in here. No windows. Do you just use that lamp?" She gestured to the green-shaded desk lamp that Morty had found in the firm's storage room years ago. He nodded. "That's nice. I like dark." Tympany then sat down in the chair on the other side of Morty's desk. She crossed her legs and Morty noticed that no fat squished out. He sat back down, as well.

"I came here from Watson & James over in Los Angeles." The top foot began to bob up and down slightly. "Great firm. Bigger than this one. I like LA better than here, but I think I'm stuck here for a while. My boyfriend got a job here, so I'm stuck. We tend to move a lot, so I'm used to it." Tympany waited for a response from Morty, but he didn't know what to say. Undaunted, she picked up the thread again. "How long have you been here?"

"Oh, uh, about ten years now. I like it here. I have lots of work." Another cough. He now began to smell the stale scent of cigarettes.

"You do litigation, right?" Morty nodded. "I do real estate. So I review title reports, legal descriptions, that sort of thing. It's pretty okay. It gets boring." Tympany picked at her left arm and it was then that Morty noticed the bottom part of a tattoo peeking out from beyond the sleeve of her tee-shirt. It looked like the bottom half of an encircled star.

Finally, Tympany left Morty's office and Morty felt relieved but unnerved for several hours afterward. He stared at the pages of documents as he lifted them out of banker's boxes, but couldn't actually read any words. At one point, Jason Schroeder, a litigation associate, poked his head into Morty's office.

"Hey, Morty, have you got the documents for the Malmott case organized yet? I'd like to take them home over the weekend." Morty jumped up and clasped his hands together.

"Oh, yes, yes, uh, they'll be done. I'm just finishing them up now."

The associate smiled, thanked Morty, and disappeared. Morty sat heavily in his chair. It was time to get a grip.

Two days later, Morty entered his office at 7 a.m., as usual, and dropped his frayed, black backpack by his chair. As he leaned over the desk to turn on his lamp he noticed something in his chair. It looked like a Christmas ornament. It was comprised of three small twigs tied together with string and had a long string attached at the top, presumably so it could be hung. Morty picked it up gingerly and turned it over in his fingers. He stared at it for a while, puzzling over it.

"Hey, Morty." A voice from his doorway startled him and he looked up. It was Jason Schroeder again.

"Didn't mean to scare you. Can I come pick up the Malmott boxes from you this afternoon? I need to review them over the weekend."

Morty nodded, looking as though he'd been caught doing something wrong. "Yeah, sure. They'll be ready." Jason gave Morty a tight smile, just a stretching of his lips, tapped the doorjamb with his fingers and disappeared. Morty quickly threw the ornament into his top drawer and began to concentrate on the Malmott documents again.

About an hour later, Morty had the eerie sensation that someone was in his office, standing behind him in the corner. He felt the need to keep looking behind him, but no one was there. His office was quite small, so it wasn't likely there could be anyone there without it being obvious, but the sensation was so persistent that Morty turned on the overhead band of fluorescent lights. It helped a little. The feeling didn't go away, but his office felt less creepy that way.

Soon thereafter, Tympany came into his office with a broad smile and plopped into the chair in front of his desk.

"It's light in here." She said, smile never wavering. "There's a lot of light now." Morty nodded and looked at her but said nothing.

"You know, Morty, I like to know things about the people I work with. I think it just makes things better that way, you know?" Morty didn't know, but he nodded anyway. "So I live with my boyfriend over on the east side of town in the Aardmoore neighborhood. It's the oldest neighborhood in the city, from what I'm told. Lots of big, old houses and big trees and lots of history. We wanted an old house. They have so much more character, don't you think?" Morty nodded again, but had no real opinion on the subject. "Do you live in one of those nice condos they just put up on the water?" Morty cleared his throat.

"No. That's not where I live."

"Oh, where do you live then?"

"In an apartment. It's small. I can't afford much more than that."

"Ah. So you don't have roommates or anything?"

"No." Cough.

"Well, living alone can be nice." Tympany smiled her big smile again. "So did you grow up around here? Do you have family? Sisters and brothers?" Morty was beginning to be palpably uncomfortable and his armpits were prickling.

"Well, um, my dad is dead and my mom is in memory care. I don't have siblings. I grew up nearby." Just answer the questions and maybe she'll leave. Tympany nodded, looking as if she might be sympathetic.

"I'm sorry about your mom and dad. That's tough." All of the sudden she lifted her feet, gave a little stomp on the ground, and popped up from the chair. "I won't bother you anymore. I see you've got a lot of work. It's good talking to you, Morty." And out the door she went, Morty staring after her as she left.

Monday morning came and Morty actually felt pretty good about the day. He had decided that he wasn't going to think any more about the Christmas ornament and that he was being silly for allowing it to bother him. He walked into his office at 7 a.m., dropped his frayed, black backpack next his chair, and leaned over to turn on his desk lamp. He saw it immediately. There was another ornament on his chair. This one, too, was made out of twigs and string, but it was crudely shaped into a person. Morty carefully picked it up by the loose string, not wanting to make a sudden move that might provoke it to attack him somehow. As he held the ornament two feet from his eyes and examined it, his office began to feel creepy again, like he wasn't alone. He quickly turned on the overhead lights and dropped the new ornament in the desk drawer on top of the other one. He slammed the drawer shut and the decisive sound made him feel a bit better.

Morty tried to focus all morning on his work, but his eyes and his mind kept wandering toward the drawer. At lunch time, he decided he didn't want to eat in his office and took his sack lunch and carton of milk to the cafeteria. He sat in a corner with an old magazine someone had left behind. Soon he thought he heard his name. He looked over and two tables away he saw Tympany sitting at a table with a senior real estate associate. Morty thought his name might be Travis.

"So how well do you know Morty Blevins," Tympany asked, legs crossed, foot bouncing, fork picking at whatever was on her plate. Travis shrugged.

"I don't, really. It's hard to know that he even exists. The litigators know him, of course, but we don't have anything to do with him in real estate."

"There are people like that." Tympany said. "It's like they never existed and no one would know if they were gone."

"Yeah," Travis agreed, "that would describe Morty." Morty shrank further into his corner. He didn't really care that Travis thought he was forgettable. It was the ominous sounding words from Tympany that bothered him. Morty continued to sit quietly in his corner until Travis and Tympany left. They never noticed him.

That afternoon, Morty spent his time searching the internet to find out as much as he could about the two ornaments he had received. He now suspected that Tympany had left them and that her tattoo was a grave clue. It took almost no time for his concerns to turn into a mild hysteria. Morty pretty quickly came across a pentagram. That, according to the internet, was the penultimate symbol of witchcraft. Morty was sure that Tympany's tattoo matched what he was seeing on his computer screen.

According to other information he was able to piece together, the two ornaments were not ornaments at all but totems used in witchcraft. Witches used totems for various purposes. Sometimes they kept one as a personal amulet as protection against evil forces. Sometimes, however, they themselves used them for evil purposes. For example, a witch might mark a future victim by leaving a series of totems near that victim. The totems were thought to eventually render the victim powerless against any of the witch's malevolent intentions. Morty read that this sort of thing was related to voodoo and hexes, as well, but couldn't bring himself to learn exactly how. He was already feeling light-headed.

That night Morty did not sleep more than a couple of hours. The next morning there it was, on his chair, another totem. He threw it in his desk drawer with the others. He got very little work done that day. He couldn't even think straight enough to do more research on witchcraft.

Later that afternoon, Morty and his black backpack climbed the three flights of stairs to his small apartment. The apartment was not furnished as one would expect of a 40 year old bachelor. It looked like a time capsule from 1978. The small living room was stuffed with a green velour couch and matching recliner, both facing a wagon-wheel coffee table. There were several walnut end tables flanking the couch and chair, with matching brass lamps perched atop. The only anachronism was a small, flat-screen television - not much bigger than a large computer monitor - sitting on a walnut stand. The apartment was filled with the furniture and other artifacts from Morty's childhood home. After his father had died and his mother had gone to the nursing home, Morty moved as much as he could into his apartment, and managed to successfully recreate the old living room. It was very comforting.

Morty turned on the television so that he could watch the local news at 6 p.m. Morty was not particularly interested in the local news, but he liked the companionship of Chad Thompson and Delia Spry, the two newscasters. Every weekday evening he could eat his dinner while they chatted at him through the television. They were nice looking and he liked the banter. They were always joshing with the weather guy. Sometimes Morty joined in a little, but only sometimes. He mainly just liked to watch them.

Morty heated up a plate of leftover spaghetti and got a can of Sprite from the refrigerator. Then he settled onto the couch, put his plate and soda on the wagon-wheel coffee table, and hunched over the plate to keep any spaghetti from falling onto the gold area rug. Chad talked about the city's new mayor and then warned of a possible increase in water and sewer rates. When he had finished, the camera cut to Delia. Next to her on the screen was a graphic that said, "Missing Cats Concern Neighborhood."

"We are now going to go live to the Aardmoore Neighborhood where Emily Small is investigating a strange occurrence in that normally quiet area." Said Delia.

"Thank you, Delia," said Emily. "I'm here in the Aardmoore Neighborhood because in the past few weeks neighbors have started to report that their cats have gone missing. More disturbingly, two mutilated cat bodies have been found. It's not clear whether there's a coyote in the neighborhood or maybe a dog that has been attacking cats, but some say the wounds on the cat remains do not look like anything another animal would do." Morty froze. The Aardmoore Neighborhood was where Tympany said that she lived.

"I have one of the neighbors here who has agreed to talk to me, but she doesn't want her face to be shown on-camera." Emily turned and the camera cut down to the bottom half of a pair of purple pants. The pants were too short and swollen ankles burst out of soft, lace-up sneakers. Morty was sure it was an old lady. "What can you tell us about the missing animals?"

"Well, I have lived in this neighborhood for over 40 years and we've never had anything like this happen before." The voice confirmed it was an old woman speaking, but a vigorous old woman. "I keep track of things in this neighborhood, so I would know. I'll tell you when it started. It started when some new people moved a couple of houses down from me. They look kind of fishy from what I have seen of them, but it's hard to get a good look. It seems like they have a lot of parties, every couple of nights or so. Well, you would think they're parties because there are a bunch of people that go into the house. But they're always real quiet. There's no music and the house is really dark inside. I don't know what kind of party that could be. Sometimes I see a red light in the attic window and sometimes a shadow passing by the window . . ." The old woman clearly wasn't done, but Emily awkwardly jerked the microphone away from her mouth mid-sentence. The camera quickly panned back up to Emily, who had a nervous smile pinned on her face.

"I don't think we should speculate too much on a particular house." Emily's voice wavered. "I think the point we want to get across to our viewers is that they need to keep their pets safe and in their houses until this mystery is cleared up. We'll certainly stay on top of this story. Back to you, Delia."

That night Morty did not sleep at all. Instead, he stared into the gloom of his bedroom until he began to feel that same creepy feeling he had felt in his office when the overhead lights weren't on. At about 3 a.m., Morty convinced himself that he was seeing flitting shadows through the gloom. He didn't know if they were real or if he was just starting to imagine things. He turned on the light and tried to distract himself with the television in his bedroom. The old black-and-white shows were better than the constant chatter in his head. At some point he noticed it was morning and got up for work.

When Morty arrived in his office, he was not surprised to see another totem on his chair. His heart beat wildly and he felt sick. He thought he smelled stale cigarette smoke.

"You're a little later than usual this morning, Morty." It was the witch at his office door. Morty stared at her. She stared back. Was she trying to feign innocence? It looked that way. "Hey, are you feeling okay? You look a little tired." She was certainly feigning concern.

"Yeth." Morty's mouth was dry.

"Well, try to get some more sleep. You do look tired. You don't want people to worry about you." She smiled and turned to leave.

"Do you like cats?" Morty was not intending to say anything more to Tympany. The voice came from nowhere, but he recognized it as his own. Tympany cocked her head and narrowed her eyes.

"What an odd question for you to ask me, Morty." A pause. "Yes, of course I like cats. See you around, Morty." She smiled again and was gone.

After she left, Morty immediately got on his computer and started searching for someone who could help him. Was there an exorcist for witches or anything like that? What were one's options when being pursued by the supernatural? After typing in a number of search words in Google maps, the name of a small store about eight blocks away came up. The name of the store was simply "Hexafoil," and the description said, "Everything you need for your adventures in the occult." Morty wouldn't really describe what was happening to him as an adventure, but this store seemed to be as good of a place as any to start.

Morty shoved the totems into his backpack and left the office, no one noticing that he had gone. He arrived at Hexafoil just as an old grizzled man, who Morty thought looked like a wizard, flipped the closed sign around and unlocked the door. The wizard opened the door for Morty and Morty stepped in.

"Well, you're certainly an early bird," he said. Morty noticed the smell first. There was an underlying musty odor overlain with all sorts of other earthy smells that he couldn't place. There were crystals, candles, books, and what looked like an old-fashioned apothecary on the wall behind the cash register. Everything looked old and dust motes floated freely through weak shafts of light from two high windows in the back of the store.

"What can I do for you, son?" asked the wizard. Morty went over to the counter with the cash register, set his backpack on top, and pulled out the totems. He handed them over to the wizard who took them with a knowing grimace and nodded his head.

"Where'd you get these?"

"I keep finding them in my office. I think I'm being marked by a witch." The wizard nodded his head again as he turned the totems over in his hands.

"Yep. I would say so. I would say someone's trying to mark you alright." Morty almost fainted. It was real! "So, what would you like to do about it, son?"

"I-I don't know. I was hoping you could help me. I want to be left alone." Morty's eyes were large and he didn't blink. The wizard seemed to think a moment.

"Okay, sure, I can help you." He said and began walking to a display of rocks and crystals. Morty followed him like a docile dog. The wizard picked up what looked like a common river rock, small, grey, and smooth. He jostled it in his hand for a few moments while looking up, squinting, trying to gauge something. He then nodded to himself and gave the rock to Morty. "Here, this should do it. We don't want to go too powerful right at the beginning. It could be dangerous if we did that." Morty looked at the wizard questioningly. "That rock will sap the witch's power. It has special properties just for that purpose. Just put it somewhere near the witch, somewhere she can't see it, and it will start to do its work. It may take a couple of days, but it should take care of the problem." Morty felt a wash of relief. Thank God. A solution.

The rock cost Morty $62. It seemed like a lot of money for a rock, but it did have special powers, and what other choice did he have? When Morty returned to the office, he waited for the lunch hour. He then slipped into Tympany's office and carefully placed the rock in a file drawer. Slipping back into his own office he almost felt giddy.

Unfortunately, that did not solve the problem. The totems continued, as did the creepy feeling, as did Tympany's occasional visits the purpose of which seemed only to track his deteriorating state of mind. The number of missing cats in the Aardmoore Neighborhood was beginning to dwindle, but most likely because people were no longer allowing their cats outside. On the next Monday, Morty was again waiting in front of the Hexafoil as the wizard flipped over the closed sign and unlocked the door. The wizard smiled sympathetically as Morty entered.

"The rock didn't work." Morty said simply, eyes rimmed in purple. The wizard shook his head.

"Well, I was hoping it would. Here's what we'll do. I'm going to give you a second rock. That will double the power and will almost certainly neutralize her powers." Morty gratefully accepted the second rock, paid the $62, and over the lunch hour placed it in Tympany's file cabinet next to the other one. A couple of days later, there, sitting on his chair, was another totem. The rocks didn't seem to be working. At 2 p.m., Tympany appeared in his doorway. She no longer sat down for these visits. She could see well enough from the doorway that Morty was not doing well.

"Hey, Morty," came the cheery voice, "I'm having a party on Saturday. Just some friends and it seems like you could use some fun, you know, let loose a bit and relax. Would you like to come?" Big smile, tilted head. Morty felt the armpit prickles again.

"No, thank you." He swallowed. The images of mutilated cats flashed before his eyes. Maybe Tympany and her friends were thinking of graduating to people, people like him, whom probably no one would miss.

"Oh, I think you should come." Sing song voice. "I think you need it. Think about it and I'll check back in with you before the weekend. I won't take no for an answer."

As soon as Tympany was gone, Morty rushed out of his office and went straight to Hexafoil. If the wizard looked surprised at all, it was only because Morty had shown up in the afternoon. Once Morty explained that the rocks weren't working and now the witch was wanting him to actually come to her house, probably to be sacrificed in a bloody ritual in her attic, the wizard looked very serious.

"This witch is more powerful than I thought." The wizard sighed deeply. "Okay, son, I had hoped it wouldn't come to this, but I think we'll have to go there." The wizard turned to the apothecary wall and pulled down an old tin cylinder. He tapped on it solemnly with his index finger. Morty noticed how long the nail was. "This is wolfsbane, some call it the devil's helmet, others monkshood. It is toxic to a witch's power. Too much and it would be toxic to the witch herself. You only need about a teaspoon." The wizard pulled a tiny zip-lock baggie from under the counter. He then opened the tin and pulled out a tiny scoop. The wizard took one scoopful of the white powder and carefully placed it in the baggie, just as carefully zipping it shut. He put the baggie next to the cash register and Morty saw him ring up $325.

"That's a lot." Morty blurted out before he could catch himself. The wizard nodded sadly.

"I know, son, but your witch is quite powerful. I wish I had an alternative for you." Morty felt the wizard was probably right and pulled his credit card out of his wallet. He didn't want to die in a bloody attic ritual.

After he had paid, the wizard instructed Morty to sprinkle the powder on something the witch would probably touch. The witch needed to come into contact with the powder for it to be effective. Morty understood and went back to the office. That afternoon, he stayed in his office until close to 8 p.m. Litigators were often in the office late and he wanted to make sure no one would see him go into the witch's office. When he felt the coast was clear, Morty put the baggie into his pants pocket and left his office nonchalantly. As he headed for Tympany's office, a senior partner came out of her office and walked past him, going in the opposite direction. Morty momentarily panicked, but it didn't appear that the senior partner had noticed him at all.

Once in the office, Morty saw a document on Tympany's desk, next to a yellow legal pad. It was a thick document with several pages flipped back over the staple and there was writing on the notepad. Clearly she was working on this document when she left and would probably resume where she'd left off when she returned in the morning. Carefully, Morty pulled out the baggie and sprinkled the white powder onto the open page of the document. If one looked closely enough at the page, one would see the powder. But if one wasn't expecting anything, the powder would be touched before it was noticed.

That night, Morty slept better than he ever had. He was strangely certain that the wolfsbane would work. In fact, he slept so well that he overslept and woke up at 9 a.m. When he saw the time he had to blink several times to be sure he was seeing the clock correctly. Morty then bolted out of bed and rushed to get ready. Even so, it was 10:30 a.m. before he reached the office. As he walked through the lobby and then the hallway leading to his office, he was aware that something must have happened. People were clumped together here and there talking and looking around. Morty was intrigued but had no one to ask.

Morty walked into his office, dropped his frayed, black backpack next to his chair, and then leaned over to turn on the desk lamp. The light clicked on with the pull chain. Morty, with some dread, looked down at his chair and was relieved to see that there was no totem on it. He smiled to himself and began to open a banker's box full of documents. He felt like humming.

"Hey, Morty." A short knock and Morty looked up to see Jason Schroeder leaning into his doorway. "I'll need another box of documents to take home this weekend."

"Sure," said Morty. Jason looked as though he was about to leave but then leaned back in.

"Weird thing this morning, huh?" he said, glancing down the hall. Morty stopped breathing and to Jason his face appeared blank. "Oh, you didn't hear? That new real estate paralegal, she died this morning. The paramedics came and everything but they couldn't save her. Anaphylactic shock, I guess. Somehow she came into contact with peanuts. I guess she was really allergic. It's not clear how she was exposed to peanuts. They'll probably test things in her office to see if they can figure it out, but, wow, huh? Life's weird." Jason then tapped the doorway with his fingers and left.

Morty looked down at the banker's box. He should probably feel bad, but he only felt empty. The wizard must have miscalculated the amount of wolfsbane needed, he thought. Morty hadn't meant to kill the witch, just make her leave him alone. Of course, he really hadn't killed the witch at all. If anyone had killed her, the wizard had, but that really wasn't Morty's problem to deal with. Plus, he didn't want a wizard mad at him now. That wouldn't do at all. At the end of the day, witches had to expect that this kind of thing could happen, especially if they were planning to kill someone in a bloody attic ritual.

Although the small amount of peanuts was easily found on the open page of the document that Tympany had been working on, no one could figure out where it came from or how it got there. They would never tie it to a tin of white powder on an apothecary shelf in an old, musty store selling the occult. And because of that, they would never see the packaging of the white powder that the store owner would occasionally pour into the tin, which, in large letters said "Big Jim's Protein Powder" and in smaller letters below: "Now enhanced with peanut powder for extra protein."

No one would ever tie the incident to Mortmain Wendell Blevins, either. Partly because the powder remained a mystery, and partly because Morty had two unlikely superpowers: he was both completely inscrutable and utterly forgettable.

WORM-SACKS AND DIRT-BACKS

Lee Clark Zumpe

The sanitary world around Dr. Kenneth Sprague had rotted away revealing its rancid underbelly.

"Who are we kidding? Reconstituted disinterred entities? The formerly expired? The prematurely lamented?" Sprague had used his last euphemism. Frustration and fatigue finally stripped him of his last ounce of professional prudence as he bickered with the chief of staff at Arnesville Regional Hospital. Surrounding the two men, the dead huddled in a once spotless hallway, many clustered in familial groups, whimpering and trembling. They had spilled into the corridors from an overcrowded and understaffed emergency room. Outside, they shambled through the parking lot, gazed despondently at their reflections in car windows and picked at their own putrescent flesh. "They're walking corpses. How am I supposed to treat walking corpses?"

"Just do your job, Dr. Sprague." Dr. Zephram Ames responded to Sprague's outburst with a cold stare and an unsympathetic tone. The 50-something physician ran the hospital with an iron fist in the best of times. The current crisis had transformed him into a fascist despot devoid of compassion for his colleagues. "I expect you to treat each one like any other patient: Examine their symptoms, manage their pain and monitor their progress. It's all that we can do until a treatment or a cure is developed."

"There won't be a treatment or a cure," Sprague said, his tone growing more insubordinate as his discontent and resentment mounted. Those who required and deserved legitimate health care were being turned away from the hospital because of the extraordinary circumstances. Sprague had not worked his way through medical school to spend the rest of his life dealing with an endless parade of moldering patients. "This isn't a disease. It's an aberration of nature."

"We have our orders." Ames referred to strict government directives outlined in a hastily drafted Presidential Executive Order shortly after the onset of the epidemic. "Our hands are tied. The law dictates our actions. I won't risk my career over this."

"And I won't waste mine medicating things that by all rights should be destroyed."

Sprague turned his back and walked down the grim corridor, navigating the ghastly tangle of fetid flesh and moaning cadavers. He longed for fresh air, untainted by the lurid stench of the dead. At the end of the hallway, he hesitated in front of a service entrance, wishing he could leave it all behind him; wishing he could ignore his conscience and go home and wait it out.

He could not help but feel beguiled by the bliss of seclusion, the promise of total tranquility as could only be achieved in complete isolation. At the same time, he feared what might become of the city – of the world – in his absence. What today manifested itself as a plague of the dead could tomorrow become a scourge of the living. He had an obligation to stay alert, to stay focused, to watch for signs of mutation.

After a moment's deliberation, he turned toward the stairwell and headed for the roof. Though he had no weather reports to notify him, he could tell a cold front was pushing through the mountains. He hoped the arctic winds would offer a temporary reprieve from the stomach-turning aroma saturating the hospital's lower levels.

Down there, everything smelled like the grave.

He had examined dozens of reconstituted disinterred entities over the last few weeks, poked and prodded them, even gathered specimens to be forwarded to the USAMRIID task force facility located on the outskirts of the city. He continually questioned the military's unprecedented utilization of civilian medical personnel to act as first responders in the outbreak, criticizing army scientists for distancing themselves from the hot zone.

Nothing about the epidemic made sense. The government's initial reaction had been to quarantine the city – a feat made feasible thanks to the area's rugged topography. Set in the Appalachian Mountains in far western North Carolina, Arnesville could be cut off from the rest of the region relatively easily with the closure of four state highways and a 20-mile stretch of the Interstate system. State police simply rerouted traffic through nearby Canton and Waynesville.

A media blackout quickly followed. All television, radio and newspaper services terminated with swift and shocking efficiency. The military apparently deployed some form of equipment that jammed external radio signals and made satellite dishes ineffective. All phones, both land-line and cellular, ceased to function. Postal deliveries were halted.

Not a single journalist entered the city after the implementation of the quarantine.

Then, instead of inserting troops to round up the infected corpses, the military positioned itself along the quarantine perimeter and set about patrolling the back country in Black Hawk choppers. No epidemiologists arrived to relieve the overtaxed medical community. No FEMA workers appeared to assess the conditions and provide logistical support. No government representatives visited to address the concerns of local residents, to offer reassurances or provide explanations and chart strategies.

Finally, word came down that the president had extended limited Constitutional rights to those affected – and that the "killing" of any such entity constituted a federal offense punishable by, ironically, death.

Unlike those in Washington D.C., Sprague had no misconceptions about the state of the "corporeal undead," the term employed to describe the entities in the official document. The dead rarely spoke, exhibited no emotion other than chronic depression and appeared to have only limited fine motor skills. He saw no spark of intelligence in their eyes, no flicker of remembrance and no internal motivation to survive. Left to their own devices, they might well waste away into nothingness: They ate nothing, drank nothing and, aside from wandering aimlessly and groaning unremittingly, they did nothing.

Admittedly, some of Ames' closest associates had achieved some success with experimental therapy. His team worked in secrecy in the upper levels of the hospital, selecting trial candidates through a careful screening process. From the notes he had shared with other staff members, the things could be nourished intravenously, taught to perform simple skills, prompted into speech.

That Ames sanctioned such trials repulsed Sprague. Those responsible for the research argued that their work was a logical extension of their scientific background. They considered themselves medical revolutionaries exploring cutting-edge rehabilitation techniques.

Sprague likened them to grave-robbers bent on harvesting the dead for their own selfish professional purposes.

"Fed up with the working conditions down there, Dr. Sprague?" Arriving on the roof, the physician found a congregation of expatriated interns smoking and sharing a bottle of Jack Daniels beneath the ruddy evening skies. "Or have you come to collect us and usher us back down to our stations?" Randy Donne had apparently been elected as the group's provisional spokesperson. The other greenhorns lacked the courage to voice their antipathy and aversion to dealing with the dead. "If that's the case, I'm afraid that we'll have to decline the invitation."

"No," Sprague said, "I'm here for some fresh air."

"Not much to go around." Donne flicked his cigarette butt over the side of the building, followed its descent with his gaze. The street in front of the hospital teemed with squirmy corpses. "There's so many of them now you can smell 'em all the way up here."

"Damn worm-sacks and dirt-backs," Freddie Julian said, downing a swig from the bottle. Sprague had heard both expressions in recent days, counted them among the more evocative inventions in an evolving lexicon. *Worm-sacks* referred to corpses over six months old, dug up by optimistic relatives and subsequently abandoned due to their advanced state of decomposition. *Dirt-backs* were the recent dead, in most cases spontaneously reawakened in the midst of their own burial. "Someone should be corralling them, herding them toward a crematorium or something."

"That's not the will of the government," Sprague said with a hint of sarcasm. Black Hawks hovered over the distant horizon, combing the countryside. Occasional weapons fire had been heard over the last few days suggesting that some citizens had attempted escape. "For whatever reason, they want to keep them intact for the time being."

"Probably want to register them for November's general elections." Donne glanced at the stars emerging in the twilight between wispy bands of clouds. To the west, a line of storms crawled along the Appalachian crest. "Why do you think they've all come here, to the hospital? Why not go to their homes, their families?"

"They're suffering physical pain," Sprague answered. "That much we know. Assuming they retain some memories of life, they associate the hospital with feeling better."

"I guess we should be thankful they aren't flesh-eating zombies." Julian - not a particularly squeamish individual - visibly shuddered at the thought of how much worse things could be if the dead had awoken with a ravenous appetite. "I mean, that's what you expect the undead to do, right? Feast on the living?"

"I don't really know what to expect them to do, Freddie." Sprague looked down upon the crowds, wondered how many had passed through the hospital doors previously on their way to the burial ground. How had the gardens of rest been transformed into the gardens of the restless? Julian's gratitude that they did not more closely resemble their cinematic representation led Sprague down another disquieting avenue of thought: With so many variables at work, so many mysteries as yet unanswered, no one could really be certain that they might not all rise up and start gorging themselves on the living. "Honestly, I don't think that they know what is expected of them, either."

The meatwagons began arriving the following day just after sunrise.

Dr. Sprague had spent the night on the roof with Donne and several other interns waiting for a squall line that regrettably stalled over the highlands. The first indication the day would be different came with the appearance of dozens of Chinooks sweeping in from the south flying low over the Pisgah National Forest. Like impatient buzzards they circled the distant Arnesville International Airport, waiting for clearance.

"It's about time," Donne said, his upturned palm eclipsing the morning sun as he followed the helicopters' flight. He imagined the transport copters filled with anxious national guardsmen, ready to take all the dead into custody and convey them out of the city. Simultaneously, a column of black panel trucks maneuvered a maze of side streets and convened along Avery Boulevard. Escorted by local police, the caravan carefully approached the hospital. Some shell-shocked residents stumbled from their homes along the thoroughfare to watch the grim procession. "Maybe they've come to their senses."

"Maybe," Sprague said, reserving judgment. "I'd better find Ames – see if I'm still employed." Before returning to the stairwell, the doctor peered over the ledge as paramilitary guardsmen escorted the first of the corpses into the backs of the meatwagons. The dead went willingly without any hint of resistance. They moved like cattle, without deliberation or reflection. "You all should get downstairs, see if you can help. When this mess is finally swept under the carpet, people will need our help again. That's why you're here. That's why you'll stay."

Sprague found Ames on the 10th floor. He had appropriated an entire wing for his team of researchers, ostensibly to investigate how best to treat the dead. Where uniformed security guards had restricted access yesterday, this morning Sprague found no obstacles.

"Dr. Ames," he called out, catching sight of the doctor down the hall. A tall, gaunt man with greasy hair and an expensive, tailored business suit conversed with Ames in front of a shadowed alcove at the far end of the corridor. From the man's emphatic gesticulations and boisterous tone, Sprague inferred a considerable degree of conceit. As the physician approached, Ames lifted a hand to curtail their tête-à-tête temporarily.

"Dr. Sprague, a pleasure to meet you," the man said, turning to face him. He contrived a disingenuous smile that unfolded across his pallid countenance like a serpent uncoiling itself to strike at some unwitting rodent. "I'm Bernard Chesterton, CEO of Therst Weber Pharmaceuticals." He began to extend his hand to cement the greeting but pulled back reflexively as if concerned about potential contagions. "I was just expressing my gratitude to Dr. Ames for his handling of this situation."

"I'm sorry," Sprague said, looking back and forth between the two men. "This just seems like an odd time to be hawking new drug treatment options, doesn't it Dr. Ames?"

"Actually, Dr. Sprague, Mr. Chesterton is here to take guardianship of our corporeal undead. His company has taken full responsibility for the situation." Everyone knew Ames received kickbacks from the major pharmaceutical companies. His zealous support of their products resulted in endless perks and enabled him to build his palatial 5-bedroom mansion on a ridge overlooking the city while paying alimony to two ex-wives. In addition to pushing unessential prescriptions on patients through hospital staff and local doctors, Ames regularly advocated and approved clinical trials for dubious medications. "Because of its culpability, the company has made arrangements to oversee the re-education process."

"I beg your pardon?" Sprague needed no clarification. As he had suspected from the onset, someone behind the scenes had orchestrated the whole depraved enterprise – and Ames had played a pivotal role. The worm-sacks and dirt-backs had been intentionally revived. "So, you aren't going to destroy them? You're going to treat those things?"

"That's right, Dr. Sprague. It's no fault of theirs' that they've been reanimated. Following a treatment regime developed and tested in part by Dr. Ames here, they will be reintegrated into society. Properly medicated, they'll continue to serve as active members of the community indefinitely."

"As what? Doorstops?"

"Come with us, Dr. Sprague," Ames said, placing a firm grasp on his shoulder as if to rein him in. "We were about to tour my makeshift recovery ward. I think you'll be surprised at the progress we've made."

Behind the guarded doors, air fresheners masked the stench of decomposing flesh. The revivified dead rested comfortably in hospital beds meant for the living. Unlike their kith and kin downstairs, these pampered examples had regained some semblance of color in their skin. They demonstrated a diverse range of palpable, though imperfect, expressions and displayed rudimentary emotions. Their arms and legs did not quiver and their fingers did not fidget. They exhibited a sense of purpose and identity.

"What have you done to them?" Sprague looked over the dead patients, flinching at their two-dimensional personalities, their deceptively sterilized appearance, their vacant stares. "You can pump them full of chemicals, but they'll never be the same – don't you see that? The spark is gone. Their time is already up. Science can't alter the processes of nature."

"Kenneth ... Sprague," a familiar voice called from out across the room. "Kenny, is ... that ... you?" Sprague went from bed to bed, searching for the speaker. He found him in the far corner, a copy of the Bible lying spread-eagle on his dinner tray. "It's ... good ... to see ... you ... Kenny."

"Uncle Howard?" Sprague's uncle had been dead for two years. The cancer that claimed him had resisted every form of treatment available at the time. Dozens of mourners had attended his funeral, watched as he was laid to rest in the mausoleum at Serenity Gardens. "This isn't possible."

"I ... can't ... explain." he said, his words punctuated by uncomfortably long gaps. Sprague stared at him wordlessly, studied the glowing flesh that should be withered and wasting away. The corners of his mouth twitched as he strained to smile. His fingers remained rigid, his arms fixed at his sides. His eyelids drooped but he never blinked. "How ... long?"

"Two years," Sprague answered, realizing instinctively what his uncle wanted to know. "It's been two years."

"Why ... am ... I ... here?" Each word, each movement had to be meticulously calculated and judiciously executed. Even with the treatment, the body processes lacked the fluid animation of life. They had degraded into clumsy mechanics, driven by an awkward automation mimicking vitality. "Why ... was ... I ... brought ... back?"

"I'm sorry, Uncle Howard," Sprague said, trying to repress both his grief and anger. "I don't know why." Sprague swallowed the heartache he had relinquished years earlier, reminding himself that the thing in the hospital bed could only be a shadow of the man he had known. "Those men can tell you why," he said, turning toward Ames and Chesterton. "Those men did this to you – to all of you."

Around the room, Ames' subjects exhibited a collective flash of recognition. Their medically-sustained solemnity deteriorated rapidly as the revelation gripped them. At once, all their misery and anguish and restiveness resurfaced. Something else emerged, too – an emotion thankfully absent until that critical epiphany washed over them. With newfound hatred, the corporeal undead struggled with the restraints confining them to their beds. They fought so violently that the adjacent skin tattered and turned a macabre shade of purple. Their glassy eyes bulged from their sockets.

Sprague recognized in their hostility a thirst for retribution, for justice and, maybe, for blood.

"Damn it, Sprague," Ames said, beckoning his private staff of assistants. Aides swarmed into the room, prepared to sedate the rebellious dead. Chesterton, savvy enough to appreciate a bad situation that might get even worse, quietly slipped out the door. "Get out of my ward, Sprague. Get out of my hospital."

Downstairs, lines of dead had formed in the corridors. They stretched through the emergency room, across the parking lot and down the sidewalk bordering Avery Boulevard. Troops crammed them into the backs of the black panel trucks which ferried them to the airport. There, more troops loaded them onto Chinooks. When filled to capacity, the helicopters lifted from the tarmac, heading east to some unknown destination.

Sprague, now unemployed, joined in the crowd of spectators watching the dead depart.

Later that evening, Sprague rested on his sofa nursing a bottle of imported Irish stout. Cable service had not yet been re-established, but local television stations had begun broadcasting live reports from Arnesville that afternoon.

Officially, an unnamed pharmaceutical company had been to blame for the epidemic. An allegedly unsanctioned five-year study of a drug said to promote longevity had gone horribly wrong. Ten towns across North America had been affected, including Arnesville. Exposure rates which should have been limited to 10 percent of the population had exceeded 80 percent. Though the root cause had been determined, the catalyst that actually triggered the reanimation of the dead had yet to be discovered.

Government troops had begun overseeing an evacuation of all corporeal dead entities from the stricken municipalities. Remote camps had been established to help treat and reintegrate the victims back into society.

At 8 p.m., the president addressed both houses of Congress. Sprague, on the verge of sleep, roused himself to watch the historic broadcast.

"Everything," the president said, "Will be ... all right." Sprague sat up and perched on the edge of the cushion. He upset the bottle as he hunted for the remote control. "My friends at FEMA ... are working with ... the military," he continued. His speeches had always suffered from his sluggish tone and staggered delivery. Tonight, though, Sprague paid closer attention to his cadence and inflection. "We welcome ... these people ... with open arms," he said, his eyes oddly unblinking. His rosy cheeks seemed too red, like someone might have applied blush just before he went on the air. "And I

... am willing ... to ask my colleagues ... in Congress," he stammered. His hands rested on the sides of the podium, completely motionless. "To grant full citizenship ... to the victims ... in return for ... five years of ... service to our country ... in the United States Armed Forces."

The camera panned across the floor of Congress. Representatives and Senators applauded with mechanical synchronicity, their expressions lacking any emotional subtext. Sprague spilled onto the floor, crawled over to the screen as he scanned the audience. Though some of the older members seemed a bit disheveled, most projected at least the semblance of life. A few, though, had only just begun the treatment. Their ashen faces, their sunken eyes, their leathery flesh betrayed their lingering putrescence. Tonight, the dead governed the living. Tomorrow, the world would know no better.

Regardless of the morning's setback, unflustered by potential impediments, Bernard Chesterton, CEO of Therst Weber Pharmaceuticals, stood among the powerbrokers, contented with his coup.

CONTRIBUTORS

Daniel M. Wilson is an English writer, former photographer, and current software developer from South-East London. He's a lover of the macabre and the futuristic and wrestles constantly with a desire to go and live in a shack in the woods.

Barry Vitcov lives in Ashland, Oregon with his wife and exceptionally brilliant standard poodle. He has had three books published by Finishing Line Press: a collection of poetry, *Where I Live Some of the Time* in February 2021, a collection of short stories, *The Wilbur Stories & More* in June 2022. and a chapbook collection of poems *Structures* in May 2024. FLP will publish a novella *The Boy with Six Fingers* in June 2025.

Sarah Archer's debut novel, *The Plus One,* was published by Putnam in the US and received a starred review from *Booklist*. It has also been published in the UK, Germany, and Japan, and is currently in development for the screen. As a screenwriter, she has developed material for MTV Entertainment, Snapchat, and Comedy Central. She is a Black List Screenwriting Lab fellow who has placed in competitions including the Motion Picture Academy's Nicholl Fellowship, the Tracking Board's Launch Pad, and the Austin Film Festival. Her short stories and poetry have been published in numerous literary magazines, nominated for the Pushcart Prize, and reached the finals of the Doris Betts Fiction Prize. She has spoken and taught on writing to groups in several states and countries, and interviewed authors around the world as a co-host of the award-winning Charlotte Readers Podcast. You can find her online at saraharcherwrites.com.

Daniel Loebl is a writer based in Amstelveen, The Netherlands. He regularly writes short stories and is working on his second novel.

Wayne Kyle Spitzer is an American writer, illustrator, and filmmaker. He is the author of countless books, stories and other works, including a film (*Shadows in the Garden*), a screenplay (*Algernon Blackwood's The Willows*), and a memoir (*X-Ray Rider*). His work has appeared in *MetaStellar–Speculative fiction and beyond, subTerrain Magazine: Strong Words for a Polite Nation* and *Columbia: The Magazine of Northwest History,* among others. He holds a Master of Fine Arts degree from Eastern Washington University, a B.A. from Gonzaga University, and an A.A.S. from Spokane Falls Community College. His recent fiction includes *The Man/Woman War* cycle of stories as well as the *Dinosaur Apocalypse Saga.* He lives with his sweetheart Ngoc Trinh Ho in the Spokane Valley.

Lawrence Buentello has published short stories in many magazines and anthologies. His fiction can also be found in several collections. He lives in his hometown of San Antonio, Texas.

Paul Stansbury is a lifelong native of Kentucky. He is the author of *Inversion - Not Your Ordinary Stories; Inversion II - Creatures, Fairies, and Haints, Oh My!; Inversion III – The Lighter Shades of Greys; Inversion IV – Another Infusion of Speculative Fiction;* and *Down By the Creek – Ripples and Reflections.* His speculative fiction stories have appeared in a number of print anthologies as well as a variety of online publications. www.paulstansbury.com

Diana Olney is a Seattle based fiction author, and words are her world. Her stories have appeared in several independent publications, and her debut novella was released last year in a collaborative book. She is also a two-time winner of Crystal Lake Publishing's monthly flash fiction contest. Currently, she is writing her first full length novel, half a dozen short stories, and a comic book series entitled *Siren's Song* that will be released later this year. Her newest tale, "Pretty on the Inside," is based on a true story. Visit her at dianaolney.com for updates on her latest nightmares.

Like just about everyone else you're likely to meet, **Kelly Hossaini** has been an aspiring writer since she learned to read. As an undergraduate student she studied philosophy in order to think big thoughts and write important things. She then became a lawyer and had to settle for writing briefs. Kelly retired from the law early to pursue fiction writing.

Lee Clark Zumpe, an entertainment columnist with Tampa Bay Newspapers, earned his bachelor's in English at the University of South Florida. He began writing poetry and fiction in the early 1990s. His work has regularly appeared in a variety of literary journals and genre magazines over the last two decades. Publication credits include *World War Cthulhu* and *The Children of Gla'aki* from Dark Regions Press; *Through a Mythos Darkly* from PS Publishing; *Children of Lovecraft Country* and *Shadows of an Inner Darkness* from Golden Goblin Press; and *Corridors* and *The Pickman Papers* from Innsmouth Gold. Lee lives on the west coast of Florida with his wife and daughter. Lee's inclination toward horror manifested itself early in his childhood when he began flipping through the pages of Forrest J. Ackerman's *Famous Monsters of Filmland* and reading Gold Key Comic classics like *Boris Karloff Tales of Mystery* and *Grimm's Ghost Stories.* In his teenage years, he discovered Edgar Allan Poe, H.P. Lovecraft, Ambrose Bierce, Richard Matheson and other masters of the genre. Lee's work often focuses on character interaction set against a pervading sense of cosmic dread and high strangeness.

Printed in Great Britain
by Amazon